Front cover:

The Divine Servant   Max Greiner, Jr. Designs
Phone: (830) 896-7919   Email: maxart@hctc.net
Website: www.maxgreinerart.com

Dedication

I love to learn and the church has been a wonderful place for me to grow up in. My life and ministry are truly the product of many people's input, and I would like to mention just a few:

I dedicate this book to my best friend and life partner Cheryl Jean. You exemplify, more than most, what I have written in this book.

To Jane Elizabeth, my daughter; your passion and beauty overwhelm me.

To John Robert; my son, I long to be with you again.

To Linus Morris who first introduced me to the way. I am eternally grateful.

To John Wimber, my mentor for 17 years, and the founder of my movement and the church I now pastor. I really miss you.

To the 2 churches I've had the privilege of spending most of my adult life leading: The Vineyard Southshore (Long Island) and The Vineyard Anaheim. I have you all in my heart.

Finally to Lynne Morris, my faithful administrator, for editing and re-editing and being patient with the process of writing my first little book. Bless you.

For further information, permissions, or to order books contact

Lance Pittluck
Vineyard Anaheim
5340 E. La Palma Ave, Anaheim, CA 92807
714 777 4777
www.vcfanaheim.com

Simple Thoughts on Leadership

Lance Pittluck

Simple Thoughts on Leadership

Contents

1   My Story

When I finished Fuller Seminary, I was told that the average pastor lasted about 4-5 years in the ministry. At the time I thought that was odd, but now I totally understand it. Well, here I am in my 30th year in the ministry!

I guess I have beaten the odds. At this time in my pilgrimage, I feel like I have something to say, not necessarily a definitive something, but something.

I want to start with my story, the journey that brought me to this point.

It's 1971 and I finally finished high school. Since I started surfing at 13, I dreamed of going to California and touring the famous surf spots. So I worked construction at Bedford-Styverson in New York for the summer and saved all the money I could. At the end of the summer, three buddies and I loaded up my mom's station wagon with our gear and headed west.

All I wanted to do was surf, and perhaps meet some beautiful Californian surf chicks. I wanted an adventure and I certainly got one! That summer was amazing as one swell after another poured onto the coast. We surfed and surfed and surfed for 3 months, traveling up and down the coast depending on where the surf was the best.

During that summer of fun, something strange started to happen. I began to meet young people who talked to me about having a personal relationship with God. This was the middle of the Jesus Movement and these were Jesus Freaks. They seemed to be everywhere I went, or maybe God was orchestrating things. I met them at parties, they would engage me in God talk, and I would even run into them out on the water as we surfed.

As the summer came to a close, my friends returned to New York, but I decided to stay. Interesting enough, my whole family moved from New York out to California because my dad relocated the headquarters of his business to Los Angeles.

As summer came to an end, the good waves seemed to become more infrequent, so I had to fill my time with other things. One fateful day I ended up at Pacific Palisades High School playing a little basketball. Hardly anyone was on the playground, but I noticed one guy playing handball by himself. I invited him to play some one-on-one hoops and he accepted. He proceeded to mop-up the court with me, earning instant respect. I had spent my life pursuing athletics and was a proud athlete. It turned out that he coached basketball.

When we were done, my new acquaintance Linus shared with me some of the same things the Jesus People had shared about having a personal relationship with God. I didn't understand what he was talking about, but I liked him and came to like his whole family.

Linus was about 10 years older than I, but we became friends. For the next year and a half we met frequently, usually combining some form of athletics with Bible study during which time Linus would pray. As I said, at first I didn't understand all this spiritual stuff. He might as well have been speaking to me in Chinese.

Then one day I had a revelation. I was driving home from Linus's house and the thought came to me: if what Linus is saying is true, it is really important! Not too profound and deep, but for some reason it caused me to pray. (As far as I can remember, I had never prayed on my own before.) I said, "God if you are there, show me yourself, and if you are not there you don't hear me anyway." I think that little prayer was inspired, but if not, it was enough for God. In a way, it changed everything. A real miracle happened. My eyes were opened. The next time Linus and I got together it all began to make sense. I somehow knew it was true.

God was real and He began revealing Himself to me. I didn't make a formal commitment to the Lord for a few months. I prayed to receive Christ at the Light and Power House on the UCLA campus. Thus began this adventure of having a real relationship with this very real God. I'm now in my fourth decade of following Him.

This happened during the Jesus Movement years and many were coming to know the Lord. I was zealous, both as a witness and as a student of the Bible. Within a year I was teaching five Bible studies a week. This isn't too impressive because if a person knew five Bible verses then, they would have been a leader. That said, this was when I did begin to love, teach and study the Bible seriously.

My plan was to go to the small Bible school that the Light and Power House had developed, but when I told my dad he was not too pleased. My dad was the CEO of an international air freight company. We came to a compromise – I would go to Pepperdine University and study religion. I ended up with a quality education from a great university and spent most of the time studying the Bible with some really sincere and dedicated professors.

While at Pepperdine, I met Jim. Jim surfed, lived in Malibu, and was really involved with the youth group at the local Presbyterian Church. We became friends and I got involved with the young people at Malibu Presbyterian Church. This was a great church with a real family feel and I received good teaching, lots of love, and healing there. When I was done with Pepperdine, they sponsored me to go to Fuller Seminary. Eight of us from that church went to Fuller Seminary that fall, which gave us a natural small group for support as we went through those years.

During my Fuller years, 1975-1979, I determined to do as many different types of ministry as possible as a sort of experiment to see where I would land. The only thing I knew for sure as I entered seminary was that I was not going to be a pastor! That looked very boring and I didn't relate to many of the pastors that I had met. I worked with Brother Andrew smuggling Bibles, worked on faith renewal teams going to revive local churches, and did more youth ministry. As I tried different things I realized that I liked working with people long term and watching what happed to them as they were transformed by the gospel. I realized pastoral ministry was right for me.

After my second year at Fuller, I received a call to be an assistant pastor at a small congregational church in Anaheim California. This was the beginning of a long run of pastoral leadership that extends to the present time. I have pastored in small, medium, and large churches, and overseen many pastors and leaders. I am currently the Senior Pastor of the Vineyard Anaheim in Anaheim Hills, California. My staff is larger than the congregation of the first church I pastored. I'll share more of my story as we go along in this modest book. I have learned some things along the way and my hope is that some of what I have learned will help you in your leadership journey. It is hard to reduce a life to a few pages, but I wanted to give you a sense of who is talking to you. I pray that you will benefit from what I have learned.

Study Questions

My Story

1.   How were you launched into ministry assignments when you first began walking with Christ? List two key people God used at crucial moments to challenge, guide, or open a new door of opportunity for you to minister to others? How did God use them in your life to get you moving in serving others?

2.   It can be a good exercise to go back and draw a timeline to show how you started and grew in ministry. Seeing God's fingerprints in your life helps you tune into what was deposited into you for the next chapter of life. Here are just a few questions to consider:

Identify the first lessons that tested your perseverance to maintain some aspect of ministry.

List the early skills you acquired which now aid you as a leader.

What events or people caused you to sense God's approval and call into His service?

3.   Disciple making was placed deeply into Lance's life by Linus, and he has been faithful to give that away over the years. What does this story provoke you to do?   Do you want to learn how to disciple rising leaders also? If so, begin to ask God to give you an eye for rising leaders.

2   The Servant

I am convinced that the greatest leader who ever lived was Jesus. He is my hero. He is the perfect man. He is the smartest and best leader that ever walked the face of this planet. The church needs to take its cues about leadership from Him.

There is much written about leadership today and lots of it is really helpful. I love to read and have read many Christian and secular works on leadership. But we must return to Jesus as our model. He is the perfect balance of truth and love. He is the perfect representation of God and man.

What do we see in Him? How does God present Him to us? The answer is simple; he is a servant. If we are going to follow Him, we too must become servants.

John 13 paints the perfect picture of Jesus and His leadership. He is in the upper room with His disciples for the very last time before His death and He wants to leave a real impression with them. He wraps the towel around His waist and bends down to wash their feet. The humblest act of the humblest servant. John Wimber, my mentor for fifteen years, said that leaders should "render humble service to the King and His people." I think he got it!

Leadership is about serving Him and His people.
Leadership is about loving people in whatever way they need to be loved. It is not about the leader. Jesus came to serve not be served. Leadership is about that great New Testament word *agape*; love that is divine, unconditional, unsurpassable, unlimited. We only approximate that love, but Jesus embodies it. That *agape* is the goal of our instruction and it is what we must model.

To love people is to serve people and to serve people is to love people.

This love is doing what is best for another, no matter what it costs. This is what Jesus was demonstrating as He washed their feet, and this is what He ultimately did on the cross.

Jesus must be the church's primary leadership model. We have to keep coming back to Him to learn, and to evaluate the ideas we have about leadership. Some of you are becoming leaders, but others of you are leaders of leaders and responsible for selecting new leaders. We must draw our leaders out of our pool of servants. If folks are not willing to serve in the simplest of ways, they are not qualified to lead in the church. One of the best ways to test potential leader's motivation for leadership is to ask them to humbly serve. If they are not willing to set up chairs or make copies for you – beware. If they are not willing to do something that nobody but God will see – beware. Always let them serve first, before you allow them to lead. Leadership is simply another form of service. It doesn't really matter whether you minister to one person in total secret, or get to speak to thousands. What matters is that what you do is done in obedience to God's call. I'll talk more about the importance of this call in chapter fourteen.

I started my trek ministering to whoever came my way as I shared my salvation story. My first official assignment given by the church was to lead a 3rd and 4th grade Sunday school class. Now I have the privilege of addressing a large congregation every week and traveling all over the world. It doesn't really matter. An old prophetic friend of mine used to say, "The pay is the same". What he meant was whether you are taking a nap or raising the dead, it's all the same if done in humble obedience to the King.

If you truly seek to serve people, God will give you authority in their lives. That is how it works. **Authority comes from ministry.** If you love people and faithfully minister to them, you will gain influence in their lives. People eventually figure out if your ministry is really about you and not about God and them.

This is not about you... it is about His glory and the people He came to redeem.

Said differently, true leaders care about His people. They are not just a means to their own ends. This is demonstrated by how leaders pray for them and how we treat them. I have found I can tell a lot about leaders by watching how they relate to those under their leadership, more than I can tell by how they relate to their superiors or even their peers.

A real Christian leader cares deeply about His people.

There is a sad and wonderful statement made by the apostle Paul in Philippians 2:19-20. He says, *"I hope in the Lord Jesus to send Timothy to you soon, that I may be cheered when I receive news about you. I have no one else like him, who takes a genuine interest in your welfare."* Good for you, Timothy! Sad for the rest of the church. Paul did not have one other leader that he could send who would take a genuine interest in the Philippians' church. That is amazing; astonishing! He had no one who really cared about them? That had to make Paul sad.

Our call is to be otherly. Not centered on ourselves. Not selfish, but humble and focused on God's agenda and on helping His people to be all they can be.

At this stage in my life my success is the success of those who are around me. I am like a spiritual grandfather. I want the mothers and fathers in the faith around me to do well, and to serve/love well. I am excited to see their children doing well in their walks with God. It's all about passing the faith on to generation after generation.

God does give power to leaders to influence others. That is part of our gift. Every gift is also a responsibility. We are called to utilize the power that God has given us to serve, help, and build up those under our charge. A heart to serve has to be foundational in everything we do.

I used to think that leadership was learned in a linear way where we learn lesson 1 to 1 million in order. Now I realize that learning is a mosaic. God teaches us in His order and it is different for each one of us. Eventually He will finish the mosaic with every beautiful piece in place, but it will take a lifetime and more.

The lessons in this book are not necessarily in order and you can learn them at many different levels. These are simply nuggets of truth that I have learned in the past four decades of pastoral ministry. Many of them I have been taught several times, but perhaps I am slower than you. Some of these you may deeply relate to now and others not. That is okay. Stick with the ones that seem to have life right now. They are most likely what the Father is doing in you in this season.

Your servant,
Lance.

Study Questions

The Servant

1.   Read Jn. 13:1-17. Who in your past has demonstrated what it means to "wash your feet"?

2.   Servant leadership is about building up those under our care.   What activity can you do this week to surprise those under your care to show that you lift them up?

3.   List seven qualities you think define what it means if you are becoming a servant leader in your church. Put them into a question like: Do people believe that you are willing to sacrifice self-interest for the good of the group? Let your leadership evaluate each other with the questions they devise.

3   Influence

Being an influence is one of the ways to define leadership. Leaders influence people. They influence how they think and what they do. I believe people are born with a certain capacity for leadership. God himself determines the scope of this, but although it is God-given, this potential can be developed or left undeveloped or even dormant. Many Christians have lots of potential for leadership but for whatever reason they don't choose to exercise it.

Influence itself is neutral. It can be for good or for evil. Hitler was a man that had great influence in his country and around the world. His influence was for evil. Influence can be pointed in any direction. When I was a young man, before I came to Christ, I was a leader, and led friends into drugs and the usual 60's debauchery. Jesus is the most influential man in history. His influence and His leadership were totally for good. Leadership gives you the power to influence people, but how you influence them is in accordance with your heart and the choices you make.

If you are looking for a leader, look at who has influence in a group of people. *Formal leadership* or *positional leadership* exists in any group. These leaders are the people who have been assigned or elected to that particular post. They may or may not be the true influencer leaders in that group of people.

Here are some good questions to discern who is an influencer:

> Who do people follow?
> Who do people emulate?
> Who do people quote?

When you start hearing someone's name coming out of a group again and again, take note, you may have a leader. It doesn't mean that person is a good leader, a wise leader, or a mature leader, but if they are influencing, they are to some degree leading.

This influence primarily happens through relationship. The deeper the relationship, the more influence that is exercised. For instance, Paul had great influence in the Ephesian church as a whole, but even more with Timothy, his son in the Lord into whom he poured his life. In my own life, I have had two primary leaders. Linus, who led me to Christ, spent much time with me for two years, and helped me lay a great foundation for my life and ministry. John Wimber, found me as a young pastor and let me into his life. For fifteen years we talked, traveled, and ministered together. Aside from Jesus, he has had the most influence on my life and ministry. Both men made a huge investment of time in a young man who was then to turn around and influence many!

Kingdom leadership usually advances one person at a time. Most of the leaders I know had a person or persons that gave them significant time and input. Paul described it like this to his son in the Lord, Timothy, *"And the things you had heard me say in the presence of many witnesses entrust to reliable men who will also be qualified to teach others."*

There is a leadership chain here. Jesus > Paul > Timothy > his sons > their sons. What we see is five generations of leaders produced by this chain. Leaders need an older leader to invest in them one-on-one.

A few years ago I had a moment of clarity. I felt the Lord was speaking to me about my purpose in life. He made it simple. First, my purpose in life is to influence people to follow Jesus and secondly to raise up other influencers. To put it in the biblical language of the great commission, I am here to make disciples and to raise up disciple makers. I am fully aware that only God can make real followers of Jesus, but somehow in His great plan He lets us cooperate and participate in their development.

Let me say one more thing to connect this with the preceding chapter. We gain influence through service. As we render humble service, people will give us place in their lives. All true authority comes from ministry. This only makes sense because the most influential man ever was the one who came to serve and not to be served. He said the "greatest in the kingdom is the servant of all."

Study Questions

Influence

1.   Can you state in one or two sentences what your purpose is? Write it out here.

2.   Leadership, according to our author, is measured by influence. One of the most important principles of this book is in this chapter. Our author said, "My purpose in life is to influence people to follow Jesus and secondarily to raise up influencers. I am here to make disciples and to raise up disciple makers." What would change in your ministry if you said this was your purpose?

3.   Not many things are as important as finding your Peter, James and John within your church. Read 2 Timothy 2:1-2. What spiritual formation tools from your past do you need to share with your rising leaders? What does this question want you to ask as a leadership team?

4   Example

Leadership is about setting an example.

Peter told the elders of the church to not lord it over those
entrusted to them, but to be examples to the flock, God's people (1
Peter 5:3). Paul told the Corinthians to imitate him as he imitates
Christ (1 Cor. 4:16: cf. 1 Cor. 11:1).

It is really true that we lead by example.

For years, I thought I had chosen a very different path from my
dad. As a young man I chose to be a pastor, while my dad was an
international business person. I believed I was very different from
him in who I was and how I chose to live my life. My dad was
very busy with work and we didn't spend that much time together
once I turned 12 until I left the house. Just recently, I have realized
what a huge imprint he made on my life. I now see that I am so
much like my dad, but just in a different field of work. He
modeled for me that to be successful I had to work hard, and I
surely have. He taught me much about being a man without using
hardly a word. I watched and saw what it meant to be a man. My
purpose here is not to judge my dad's influence and how good or
bad it was, but to show that he had a huge influence on me by
being who he was and doing what he did.

If you are a leader, people watch you. They watch you when you
are on and when you are off. They watch what you do as much as
they listen to what you say. They try to figure out if the two
match. This can be a hard reality! They watch you when times are
good and when times are really rough. They want to know if you
really believe what you say and if you live it.

In 1977, we lost our 3-year-old son, John Robert, to a strep
infection. It was by far the hardest thing we, as a family, have ever

gone through. When this happened, we were pastoring a Vineyard church in New York.

I could feel the people watching and waiting to see how we would react. Would we be able to trust God in the midst of this tragedy? Would we survive and still lead them? I could feel their fear and their watching eyes. You see, we don't get to be leaders only in the good times, we get to live our lives in front of lots of people. Leadership is life in a fish bowl! By the way, we survived and by God's grace we came through the other side of that experience. God's grace truly is sufficient for anything He allows us to experience.

So, understand that people watch you. They will imitate you if you are a leader. They will pick up how you view life, even the small things that seem insignificant.

Steve Nicholson, the pastor of the Evanston Vineyard in the Chicago area, tells a funny little story. He started noticing that the young men he was training were walking around as they ministered, praying with one hand, keeping the other hand in their pocket. Many of them were doing it and he thought it was strange. He finally realized that was exactly what he did. He put a hand in one pocket and used the other to pray for people. So beware of what you do!

People will remember who you are even more than what you say. I was in New York for almost fourteen years, I spoke to that church hundreds of times in many different settings, and I hope that some of my words will be remembered. But I know this: those who were part of the Southshore Church while I was there will remember me and what I was like, for good or for bad. This means you must embody the truth you are communicating. If you are trying to communicate that the Christian life is about continual growth, you must be a person that is growing. They will do what you do. Modeling is key to imparting the Christian life. We must be something before we can lead something. We will reproduce after our own kind. I call this the *Rubbing Off* principle. We rub off on each other. Our example as leader of our group sets the tone.

I want to keep growing and learning and changing and modeling what an authentic follower of Christ looks like.

If you are around people long enough they will figure out what you are really into. They will see what you really care about. You will reproduce who you are, not who you think you are, or who you pretend to be. Our leadership is not by force or coercion. We lead a volunteer army and we can only lead by example.
I have had many models in my life:

- Linus modeled for me evangelistic zeal.
- John modeled an amazing balance of life in the Spirit and extreme pragmatism about the church.
- My dad modeled the value of hard work.
- My mom modeled the beauty of relationship.
- My wife has modeled steady faithfulness.
- Jesus is the prototype of the Spirit filled man, and the perfect model of a leader.

I am thankful for all their examples!

Study Questions

Example

1.   What we do speaks louder than what we say. Our people watch us more closely than we think, in good times and especially in the bad. What are the most important things you want to rub off on the people entrusted to your care? Make a list of at least seven things you want them to catch. Once you have your list, prioritize them in the order of importance to you.

> 1.
> 2.
> 3.
> 4.
> 5.
> 6.
> 7.

2.   As you look over your list, what questions do they ask of you? Circle the ones your people would say you do as opposed to those that are just preferred.

3.   We reproduce after our own kind. Modeling is part of discipleship. This could be a good exercise for you and your leadership. Discuss how you can bring more of the seven priorities above into your weekly schedule with your rising leaders.

5 Listening

Pastor Jack is a leader of leaders. He is using the remainder of his life to pass on to younger leaders what he has learned. He does this through conferences, a seminary, and pastoral consultations where about 30 leaders gather for a week and sit at his feet (metaphorically). I was attending my second consultation when he began to open up the parable of the sower to us. He pointed out that the whole story was about **listening**! I had never thought of the parable this way and it started me thinking about how important it is to listen in the Christian life and especially in leadership.

First of all, let me say that I believe God speaks to us today. He speaks to us primarily through His Word, the Bible, but He also communicates to us by His Spirit in many different ways.

Listening to God is a primary focus for a Kingdom leader. We are to wait on God and get input and leading and instruction from Him daily. I personally try to spend time every day sitting quietly with the Lord and asking Him to speak to me in whatever way He wants. Sometimes He is very quiet, we just sit together, and sometimes our times are rich in revelation.

Leadership is about hearing from God, following Him yourself and calling others to follow too.

God wants to lead you so you can lead others. He wants you to hear from Him so you can speak to others. Ephesians 5 teaches us that Jesus is the Head of the church. That means that He is the initiator in the church. We get our direction from Him. He is the ultimate leader and we are the followers. As followers, we must learn to listen long and well.

God blesses what He initiates. So our first job is to pray and to seek and to knock until He speaks to us. We need to sit in the listening room before we launch into action. In our society today, this is a hard thing to do. We want to get on with it. Just do it! But as leaders in His Church, we can waste an enormous amount of time doing "good things" that the Father is not doing.

The Father is always at work, we just need to spend time tuning in to what He is doing and not go with what we want him to be doing. That was even true of Jesus; the ultimate leader.

So we must learn to be listeners who follow.

We have to be under authority, God's and those God has placed over us, before we are given authority. At one point in my ministry, I was overseeing many churches on the east coast of the US. One particular pastor was giving me a really hard time. In frustration, I called John Wimber to get his input. He said to me that the way that pastor was relating to me was a good indicator of his relationship with God. It took me a while to take this in, but he was really right. How we relate to our God-given authority figures is how we relate to God. We must learn to submit and obey, but for many of us that is extremely difficult.

Jesus, as the Head of the church, has the perfect plan for you, those you lead and the whole church. It is very wise for you to make it your first priority to seek Him and His ways.

Listen before you act.

Study Questions

Listening

1.   Read Mark 4:1-20. Jesus said, "If you can't understand this story, how will you understand all the others I am going to tell?" What does this parable teach about listening? Why is it so important for Christ's leaders to understand?

2.   This chapter introduces the importance of centering our day with God. It begs the question -- How do you spend time each day with the Lord asking him to speak to you in whatever way he wants?

3.   God blesses what he initiates. Leadership is about hearing from God, following Him, and calling others to do the same. It's about intimacy and friendship. How are you <u>regularly</u> retreating as a leadership team to pray, plan, and envision the future? How are you structuring listening prayer as a spiritual discipline into your people's life style?

6   Vision

Leadership is about seeing the BIG PICTURE.

LEADERS SEE THE FOREST AND THE TREES.

The higher the level of leader, the bigger the picture he sees. This is what I call *scope of ministry*. Two people can have the same gift, but with very different scopes. The one with the bigger scope will have wider vision and will affect more people with their gift.

Leaders see what God is doing corporately, not just in individuals. They can discern God's heart for a group of people. This may sound a bit too mystical, but I believe every group, organization or church, has a corporate heart and a corporate culture. It involves what the people think, what they value and what they actually do, that is, their priorities. We see Jesus addressing this reality in His words to the seven churches at the beginning of Revelation. He is not so much addressing individuals, as He is the body of the church and what is happening to the corporate whole. Leaders see the whole, and a leader's job is to influence the whole. In order to do this, the leader needs to have some idea of where the group is to go and what it is to become. This is where vision comes in. Leaders must have a vision for the future. They must know where they want to take the group. This is a picture the leader is holding in his or her heart and working toward. This picture becomes more and more detailed as you progress. Remember, I said that leaders not only see the forest, but also the trees. As you grow in leadership, you will have more and more of a clear picture for the group you are working with.

How does vision form?

I believe the simple answer is that it accumulates over time in our hearts and mind. When I first entered the church at 19, I came as a

22

young man, unfamiliar with her ways. The church was a strange mystery to me. I liked the people, but what they did seemed really weird. Why did they like singing those old songs from a book, listening to some guy in a robe, and standing and sitting endlessly? Why did they have to dress up to do that? (I was a young surfer boy saved in the Jesus Movement and the church gave me culture shock!) Now many of the churches are more culturally current. All that to say my idea of the church was naïve and uninformed. Fast-forward 30+ years and I have been in and around the church a lot.

I have seen great churches and not so great churches. I have experienced much that was wonderful and much that I could have done without. This has led me to have my current vision of my dream church. My vision has accumulated over the years as I have studied the Bible, listened to the Spirit, and seen things that resonate with my heart and things that do not. With each experience of the church, I have been making a list of things I like and things I don't like. I have stored away in my heart things I would like to do if I were ever in charge and things I wouldn't like to have. All this adds up to vision. Part is given directly by God and part comes indirectly through our experience of the church. At this point in my own development, my picture of the ideal church, my vision, is fairly detailed. For instance, I have a clear picture of what worship would look like in our celebrations. When we hit that mark it is very exciting to me and when we don't, I keep working and praying. Leaders are always working and influencing toward their true vision, the one that is deep down in their heart. It is what they truly care about. So formation of our vision is a lifetime process. It changes and grows as we mature.

One mistake I have seen younger leaders make is to try to borrow vision wholesale from another "successful" leader. This is not all bad, it is good to learn from everyone we can, and imitation is a great way to learn, but..... you are unique, your group is unique, your community is unique, and what God wants to do through you and your people is unique. You will fail if you simply try to copy what another leader does. You are not that person, and you do not have the same grace package so you can't do exactly the same thing. Beware of borrowed vision!

As Christian leaders, we are not free just to make up a vision. Our leader, Jesus, had a vision and that sets the parameters for our vision. His vision simply involved the Kingdom and the people of the Kingdom; the church. There is much taught in the NT about the nature of that Kingdom and its people. This, of course, must inform our vision at every point. Our goal is that our vision should reflect His whole counsel. This is a lifetime journey.

How did Jesus teach His vision?

He proclaimed it, explained it, and demonstrated it. He proclaimed it simply by announcing that the Kingdom (the rule and reign of God) is here or near. He told us to change and adapt to its coming reality. He explained it mostly with stories. He said things like, "The Kingdom of God is like…." Stories are a great way to impart vision. Through them, we communicate some aspect of the Kingdom that we want to emphasize. Jesus demonstrated His vision by what He did. He spent an enormous amount of time healing folks of all kinds of problems. Through these works of power, He demonstrated the nature of the Kingdom, and the name of the King. Jesus' vision for the church is for it to be a hospital where people can come as they are and meet the Great Physician. Our God is the Lord God who Heals. Our communities should reflect His healing love.

A leader must personify the vision. Jesus personified the vision of His Father. Whatever you want your group to be and do, you have to be and do also.

There are three things I want to constantly embody and pursue. I call them "the 3Cs."

Communion - I want to model seeking the Lord constantly, and to grow deeper in my relationship with Him.

Community – I want to be a relational leader in the midst of the people. Our God is not distant and out of touch and I don't want to be either. The goal of our instruction is love, and we must embody a true love for our people.

Commission – God has given a great commandment and a great commission. In my prayers and my daily life, I want to exemplify love for those that don't yet know God.

We will reproduce after our own kind. Whatever you are, you will reproduce it if you lead a group long enough. You need to *proclaim* the vision, but also *explain* the vision and *live* out the vision in your life.

This is how a leader imparts the vision of a *preferable future* (one way of defining vision) to his or her people. We model it and live it in front of them. We impart the vision by proclaiming it, explaining it and by demonstrating it with our passionate pursuit of it. Don't be naïve, your people will eventually figure out what you are really into. They will see it in your priorities, in how you spend your time, energy and money.

One final caveat: There are things that modify your vision.

One day I was really discouraged, so I got on the phone to my mentor, John Wimber, to seek some advice. I moaned and groaned about the type of people that we were gathering at the time. They came in so broken and immature, it took forever to get them functional, never mind to a place of leadership. John patiently listened to my ravings, and then he said something that has stayed with me ever since. "If you have oak, build with oak, if you have bamboo, build with bamboo." He was trying to get me to be content with what God was doing through me, and to realize that the building material can determine what type of building can be built.

The type of people you are given to work with can and even should modify your vision.

Harry works with a small group of very poor and broken people in the inner city. Many of them have been on welfare for much of their lives. He faithfully gives himself to them, and they are growing and slowly maturing with some major setbacks, but he cannot build fast. He can't multiply his leadership quickly with a group of people that are just becoming functional in their life skills.

Our dreams have to match His dreams for us.

Our vision will only become a reality if it is what He is doing. So dream on! Sit at His feet and let the Head give you His dream for your life and ministry! His dream for you will always be the best and beyond anything you could possibly see or imagine!
I am sitting here an enormously blessed and grateful man. My vision for my life was very small when I came to the Lord. I assumed I would be dead by now. God had a bigger and better . plan. I now lead a large church and get to travel all over the world proclaiming and demonstrating the Kingdom. I have been a vital part of a thriving movement of churches. It has been my privilege to witness God raise up the Vineyard and spread it throughout the world. God is good, and He had way more vision for my life than I could have ever had. All I can say is God is good........ Dream with Him.

Study Questions

Vision

1. How do your dreams reflect God's vision for His church? How would you define the corporate heart of your church? What is working to help you achieve this vision? What is not working?

2. How do you impart vision to your church? Lance used the three C's. How do you proclaim your vision clearly so your people can share it? How do you explain it through story? And how are you demonstrating it in your own actions?

3. As a leadership team, discuss three things that need to be modified right now to reach your vision as it evolves?

    1.
    2.
    3.

7   Potential

How many times have we heard, "He has a lot of potential"? In some way or another, we can say that about every person on the planet, but we usually mean it about bright young people who look like they have a lot to offer this world. Unfortunately, not everybody who has great potential reaches it. I have seen so many young Christians full of zeal and dedication drop out of the race after a few years or even months. The same thing happens with young leaders. Not many young leaders reach their full potential.

There is a Greek word I have come to love, *telos*. It means something that has reached its desired end or its potential. *Telos* is sometimes translated *perfect*, *complete* or *mature*. God desires all of us to reach our *telos*. This is particularly important for leaders because they have the potential to influence so many others.

The question is, "What determines whether a leader will reach his or her full potential?" I have been thinking about this for a long time as I have watched some make it long term in leadership and some drop out.

I have come up with a little formula. (I recognize that it is not this simple, but I am confident that these qualities are at least a big part of the equation.) So here is my formula thus far: $L + C + D + S = LTF$.

L is for Leadership – The person is called and gifted to lead. I say gifted to lead, because there is a gift of leadership in the Romans 12 list and it is so important to know God has called us to do what we are doing. There are too many hard things for leaders to negotiate, so they must know in their heart that they are where God wants them to be and doing what He has for them to do.

C is for Character – The leader is maturing in integrity and humility.

D is for Discipline – Leaders need to be willing to work hard. I have yet to meet the leader of a good-sized ministry that doesn't work really hard.

S is for Skill – To lead requires wisdom. Leaders have to learn how to build a church or a group or a company. Much of leadership is an art. Generally, we feel our way through it. But we have to come to some pragmatic understanding of how things work in the real world or the real church.

All this adds up to **Long Term Fruitfulness (LTF).**

Basically, the formula could include everything in this book, but this is a good start.

I would encourage young leaders to seek the Lord about their calling and test out whether they have a gift to lead people. There are no leaders without followers. If no one wants to follow you, you probably are not a leader.

Character is key and is the main requirement that the New Testament makes upon a leader. I will give a whole chapter to this later.

There are many disciplines that build a leader, but I will just mention two.

Leaders do need to be readers. They should be in a constant learning posture. Secondly, and a huge priority, is the development of a prayer life. A leader's first duty to their people, before even speaking to them, is to pray for them. To be a leader with any depth, one must give time to a personal prayer life.

You have to have skills! There are so many things to learn about being a leader, from how to study the Bible, to how to counsel, to how to manage an organization. There is an endless array of skills that will help you succeed.

The goal of being gifted to lead, developing character, exercising discipline, and sharpening skills is to form flourishing fruit that will remain in us and in others. You want to influence as many people to be dedicated followers of Jesus as you can. For some that will be tens, for some hundreds and for the rarely gifted ones perhaps thousands. All God cares about is you reaching your potential, your *telos*! You and I are not competing against anyone; we are just trying to fulfill the call of God on our lives. My prayer is that if you are reading this you are receiving a realistic view of what it takes to be a leader that lasts and produces much fruit.

Study Questions

Potential

1.   Lance discusses the importance of having a lifetime perspective for ministry and professional development. He sites two key convictions for his leaders. They are to maintain a learning posture and keep a priority of prayer. Create a spiritual checklist for leaders in your church. Identify at least five areas you think are mandatory for lifelong fruitfulness in everyday life.

     1.
     2.
     3.
     4.
     5.

2.   Over time Lance has developed a common set of elements that are in leaders who reach their full potential. Leadership + Character + Discipline + Skill = Long Term Fruitfulness. Read 1 Timothy 4:6-16. What else does it suggest a good servant does? List them out.

3.   Use the spiritual checklist that you came up with in question one to evaluate yourself. Who are you committed to for mentoring? How are you being mentored in a more dynamic ministry philosophy? How often do you seek repeated times of personal renewal and prayer?

8   Pain

I should have known! My leader is called the *Suffering Servant*.
Paul talked all the time about his pain. He said, "I want to know
Christ and the power of His resurrection and the fellowship of
sharing in His suffering" (Phil 3:10). All the apostles suffered
pain and all but one experienced eventual martyrdom. Look at the
Old Testament prophets and see how their lives were full of
hardship. I should have known that the life of a Christian leader
would involve a certain amount of pain. But, as a young American
Christian, I didn't understand that. When we identify with Jesus,
we get a wonderful inheritance, and some pain. Not all things are
equal. I've seen some leaders suffer unbelievably and some to a
lesser degree. But no legitimate Christian leader gets to avoid pain
in their life. We who are called to lead are called to a full life,
which includes a strong dose of pain.

I have not been exempt from pain. My four decades of ministry
have been full of wonderful surprises, but also full of excruciating
pain.

It started as a run of the mill sickness. On Thursday, we took our
3-year-old son, John Robert, to the doctor and were quickly told he
had the flu. It was going around but he would be over it in 3 – 4
days. No big deal.

We took him home, put him to bed and began to watch over him
like any parent would. On Saturday night, he began to breathe in a
shallow, labored way.

Late that night, his eyes rolled back into his head and he died!
Wow! What a shock! We rushed him to the hospital, but the staff
could do nothing. Apparently, he had caught a strep infection,
which had turned septic, and actually killed his organs. We are
still not exactly sure what happened. Nothing competes with this
as being the rawest pain that our family has ever experienced. We

were a mess. But there was the church. Thirteen years before, we had planted a church in New York that had thrived and we had gathered a significant amount of people around us.

We were in pain like never before. One of the really hard things for us was to go through this in front of people. We could feel them watching us (as they do with leaders) and asking, "What will they do with this?" "Can they survive this?" "Will they be able to trust God through this?"

I clearly remember being at my son's memorial service a few days after he died. The worship team started to play and I realized that I had a decision. Everything within me wanted to quit life and ministry. I had to choose to live and go on and be a worshipper of God at that moment, which I had very little understanding of. I couldn't sing, or I would burst out crying. So I simply chose to raise one hand unto the Lord. I was saying to Him, "I will continue. I will trust you and lean not on my own understanding."

My wife told me later that when John died, some naïve childlike faith died in her. She always thought that if our backs were against the wall and we were really in trouble, God would come and rescue us at the last moment. He didn't, and her faith was changed forever, and so was mine. Our faith is simpler now. Maybe more like Job's. Now I am learning to trust Abba, no matter what life or ministry brings. "Though you will slay me, still I will trust in you." There are no guarantees.

If you look at the heroes of the faith in Hebrews 11, some did great exploits and some were sawn in two. All were men and women commended for their faith. Don't believe the teachers who try to convince you that if you believe God enough, it will be all happiness and no pain. That is not how leadership is in the fallen world. We live in a war zone!

What are some of the typical ways we suffer and which cause us pain?

1.   There is the *simple burden of watching over people*. Paul talks about the "Burden of the churches." True Christian leaders don't have a casual, professional distance from their people. Paul talked about having the Philippians "in his heart."

If you care about people, it will cause you some pain. As you know, some do well and others fall back. We are called to rejoice with those who rejoice and weep with those who weep.

It is hard to watch your people at times and see what they go through. This is the burden of love. True love doesn't keep a wall between you and your people. You truly care about them and want the very best for them. When you see them make decisions that you know won't go well, it is hard to watch. You can speak to them, but you can't make them listen, and you can't make the decisions for them.

2.   There is *our personal pain*. It may be a prolonged sickness, or injury that you have to endure. It may be a family problem with a spouse or a child. Again, this is compounded by the fact that you have to do it in front of your followers. There is a lot of pressure on leaders in the Body of Christ to try to be perfect, to have perfect lives and perfect spouses and perfect children. The problem is that there aren't any perfect leaders.

There are real, genuine leaders that are authentic in their faith and are really seeking the Lord. But there was only one perfect one, and He has been gone for two thousand years. So cut your leaders some slack. I like to tell my church to give each other a little grace and space. We are all in process.

3.   There is *emotional pain*. I have a friend, a real leader in the Body of Christ, but he has been anxious and depressed for the past

two years. He is a very zealous guy and I think he is partly just worn out. He is not very good at pacing himself, and has bought into the lie that it is "better to burn out than rust out."

I don't think our Shepherd wants either for us. The problem with us leaders is that we are human. We go through all the undulations of a normal, human life. We fight with fear, anxiety, depression and every other human condition. If you read church history, it has always been like this. Men of great stature, like Spurgeon, and Martin Luther, had great ongoing battles with depression. In this fallen world, we all have weaknesses. As leaders, we tend to be hard on ourselves and want to live only on the upside of life. When things get rough, it can be doubly discouraging because we start to *should* ourselves, feeling like I *should* be more mature and more victorious. I'm starting to understand that Jesus is my friend who walks through all of my pain with me. He is the God of all comfort. There is no need for comfort if there is no pain!

4.   Leaders all experience *abandonment and betrayal*. Psychologists say that betrayal is one of the hardest experiences of our lives, and leaders cannot claim immunity. Think about the pastor of a large church in Southern California. A church consultant told me recently that large churches lose between 10 – 30% of their attendees per year. Honestly, many of them come and go without the leader even knowing. But among them are people that were part of the committed core of the church and their absence is noticed. It is not that they leave, but that many times they do not leave *pretty*.

When I first arrived on the scene at the Vineyard Anaheim, it was quite a mess. The previous pastor had disqualified himself and the founding pastor died three weeks after I arrived. Things were bleak. In the midst of this, people were leaving like rats off a sinking ship. I remember one particularly painful letter. It was eleven, single-spaced pages that held me responsible for the whole 20-year history of the church. Objectively, I knew I was not responsible, but it still hurt. As a leader, we can sometimes be the targets for our group's unhappiness, even if it makes no sense at all.

Betrayal, abandonment, and criticism are all part of the pain of being a leader. Think about it. Jesus was betrayed and abandoned by his best friends at his most crucial moment. He was criticized by the religious leaders and even his own family didn't completely get him.

These are just some examples of the pain that comes to every leader. What is God doing in the middle of all this? We know that Romans 8:28 says, "God takes all things and works them together for our good." We are the ones who love him and we are "called according to His purpose." Sometimes we don't see what that *good* is. In Romans 8:29, Paul tells us exactly what that *good* is. The *good* is our destiny. It is what God is doing in the life of every leader. He is transforming us into the image of his Son. He takes the good and the bad that comes our way and uses it for the good of becoming more and more like His Son. So be encouraged, nothing is wasted in God's economy. We may have to trust Him, as we may not see exactly how it all fits together. Yet, be assured, God is using the hard things you experience for a wonderful purpose. He is making you like Himself (see Hebrews 12:1-13).

Many leaders that I meet are surprised when they experience pain and resistance in their life. Don't be surprised! It is normal in life and even more normal in leadership.

One morning, in a season of pain, I was praying and I believe the Lord spoke a phrase to me. I heard him whisper, "Pain is preparation." At first, this really scared me, but it rang true. I thought of Hebrews 12, and I thought of Jesus being prepared through pain. I thought of Paul sharing in His sufferings, and I thought about my own life. God has used pain repeatedly to change me, humble me, mature me, mold me, and make me more holy. At times now, I can even thank God for the pain in my life and ministry. One thing I know is that His grace really is sufficient for whatever He allows us to experience in this life.

This was a hard chapter for me to write. I am a Vineyard pastor who believes in healing. There is a certain paradox here. All I can say is that both are true: He is the Lord God who heals, and the God of all comfort and grace, and yet, we are mysteriously called to fill up the sufferings of Christ. If I had left out this chapter I would not be telling you the real deal.

Grace and peace to you!

Study Questions

Pain

1. The author shares how God uses times of joy and times of hardship. He can use pain to humble us, mold us or allow us to share in his transforming suffering. Pain has purpose, but it also can carry confusion. If you are not careful, pain will steal your trust in God. What are the lies you believe about pain? Circle the ones that cross your mind. How do these lies affect you?

    1. Pain is always good.
    2. Pain is God's punishment.
    3. You're weak if you admit pain.
    4. Pain is not productive.
    5. It is to be avoided.
    6. It can be avoided by acting like it does not exist.
    7. God wishes us to be painless!
    8. Good Christians don't experience much pain.
    9. Pain from the past doesn't influence me today.
    10. It is unnecessary to examine the pain from the past.
    11. I will come to understand the reasons for all my pain.
    12. If you love your people, they will not hurt you.

2. Find a trusted friend in ministry and discuss the following sources of pain. Remember that your spouse also needs an outlet to address these issues with you if you are married.

    1. If you care about people, it will cause you some pain. List the people or situations that have wounded you deeply.

2. At what points in your ministry life did you feel like giving up? Who or what caused it? What kept you going?

3. When did you feel the deepest betrayal in ministry?

4. List the times sickness, injury, or family problems have taken away your confidence to lead, love, or trust God.

3. Ask your leadership team the following questions:

    1. Why is pain an important part of ministry life?
    2. What are some typical ways we suffer and experience pain in ministry?
    3. What lessons has pain taught you?
    4. What questions has pain left you asking?

9   Thanks

Attitude is everything. I used to hear Robert Schuller say, "Attitude determines altitude."

I agree that attitude has a huge amount to do with the abundance of our lives. Two people can be in the exact same circumstance; one will moan and grown, and the other will be filled with joy. What is with that?

I have to admit some verses in the Bible scare me because I'm not sure they are attainable. 1 Thess. 5:16-18 is one of them:

*"Rejoice always; pray without ceasing; in everything give thanks;
for this is God's will for you in Christ Jesus." (NAS)*

Who does that? Who lives in that reality constantly?

I have to admit two things. On the one side, I have a lot to be thankful for. On the other, I have a really hard time living out these little phrases. Perhaps it's because I grew up in New York, where at times the native language is sarcasm and negativity? Perhaps it is because I grew up in a dysfunctional family? Maybe it's my *old man* dragging me down again?   Part of our sinful nature is how we talk. Our mouth expresses our heart. Nevertheless, I am trying to find out how to live in gratitude.

Don't get me wrong, I am a tremendously blessed man. I came to know the Lord when I was 19, and that completely revolutionized my life! I have been given a beautiful, faithful wife and a daughter who I would die for. I have an abundance of material possessions, none of which I have sought after. The Lord has just poured them upon us as we have sought his Kingdom first. I even have a Harley Davidson (and she is beautiful)! God has placed me in a position of influence and respect and great fruitfulness beyond anything I could have ever imagined when I first knew Him. I have had the privilege of watching a movement of His Spirit, called the Vineyard, emerge right before my eyes. I could go on and on!!! My point is I have so much to be thankful for and yet I still struggle to stay in a constant posture of thanksgiving.

As I write this, I am working on a spiritual discipline. I am choosing to focus my prayer life exclusively on thanksgiving. They say it takes thirty days to form a new habit. So for thirty days I am living in daily gratitude. Every day I come before him and literally list at least twenty things I am grateful for. This helps me to focus on the positive. I am trying to live out Phil. 4 : 8 , which says, *"Finally, brethren, whatever is true, whatever is honorable, whatever is right, whatever is pure, whatever is lovely, whatever is of good repute, if there is any excellence and if anything is worthy of praise, let your mind dwell on these things."*

Let's be real. There is plenty of negativity to focus on in this world if you choose to dwell on it. In the group you lead, there are always good things and bad things, people doing well and people really struggling. We need to learn to focus on the positives. We have to learn to dwell on what the Father is doing in our midst. What He is doing, not what we wish He was doing, or want Him to be doing. In every group, there are things worth focusing on and encouraging people where they are at, and not merely where they should be.

There are always negatives. You can drive yourself crazy focusing on the few problems of people (and we all have them) or what has not happened yet. I know all that, but it is a battle, I think a literal battle between the flesh and the spirit, the Kingdom of God and the kingdom of darkness. We do have to choose constantly! I really want to be a grateful, positive person, but it doesn't come naturally to me. God has been so very gracious to me and I need to remember constantly all he has done. He is the source of every good and perfect gift.

If anything is good and praiseworthy in the group you lead or in your life, it is from Him. Jesus taught us that we can do nothing without Him (Jn. 15). If I could just remember and believe that, it would humble me and make me extremely grateful. So count your blessings.

The Father is always at work, so focus on what He is doing.

Lately I have even had occasions where I was able to thank Him for the hard things in my life's journey. I know that is right and real. I hope to someday live my life giving thanks in everything. Take some time and look back at your leadership story and thank God for what He has done and even more, who He has made you to be.

One final word. Your attitude is contagious. Those you lead will adopt and imitate your attitude. If you want a group with a lot of sarcasm and negativity, be that in front of them. You get the point. Who you are as a leader will be replicated among your group if you are with them long enough. If you can grow into a positive, encouraging, loving person, it is likely that many will catch that from you.

So my commitment is that I am going to keep practicing giving thanks until it permeates all of my life and I am a truly grateful and gracious man.

Study Questions

Thanks

1.   Read 1 Thess. 5:16-18; James 3:7-10 and Phil. 4:4-9. There is plenty of negativity to focus on in this world, but the secret is to learn how to dwell on what the Father is doing in our midst. Since God does not always change our circumstances, what might he need to change in you so that contentment or gratefulness would be possible?

2.   Try living in daily gratitude for some set period of time. How many days will you try working on the spiritual discipline of exclusive thanksgiving in prayer? Start to draft a list of things you are grateful for during this time. Meditate on the verses mentioned above.

3.   Who on your leadership team could join you in this exercise of exclusive thanksgiving? There is a war going on between our "flesh and spirit" for this risky and daring undertaking. What purpose could this hold for your church as an exercise in the future? Lead the way first. Let God speak to you his passion, then teach what he gives you to your group or church.

10 Prayer

One morning as I was praying, I heard the Lord whisper to me, "Fill the Church with prayer." At first I assumed it was for our church and we needed to increase our prayer. But since that time, I have been in many different contexts where the Lord has prompted me to deliver that word again and again. I believe that God wants every Christian to mature into a vital prayer life, but it is extra critical that the leaders of the church set an example in this area. We are in a unique way set aside for the ministry of the Word and prayer.

We are modeling spiritual life to those who follow us. We can't give away what we don't have. We can't point the way to something that we have not experienced ourselves.

- An honest reading of Scripture quickly teaches us the priority of prayer.
- Church history again points us to the necessity of prayer.

Richard Foster writes correctly, "All who have walked with God have viewed prayer as the main business of their lives." (*The Contemporaries Meet the Classics on Prayer,* page 17). He then lists many of our heroes of the faith and what they did in the area: Jesus, David, the Apostles, Martin Luther, David Brainerd, George Fox and many others. All of them thought prayer was a huge priority.

Paul, instructing the young leader Timothy, prioritizes prayer as number one.

"First of all, then, I urge that entreaties and prayers, petitions and thanksgivings be made on behalf of all men." (John 1:4).

Has the modern church caught that priority?

As leaders, we are first followers of our King.

If we are trying to be disciples, apprentices of Jesus the Christ, we will not get there without this ancient path of prayer. Our God is calling all of us to connect with Him in a deep and meaningful way.

Listen to Paul as he writes to the Colossians:

"Devote yourself to prayer, being watchful and thankful"

We are to commit ourselves to learning how to pray. We are to make a devoted priority of prayer. Devotion takes discipline. We must build this into our schedules. I know that we know this, but I am constantly surprised at leaders and how little they give themselves to this devotion. When I get with them and ask them to be honest, many confess that they have no real time alone with the Lord in their regular schedule. To be watchful is to be aware in two directions. We need to become tuned-in and aware of the Father,who is always at work.

On the other side, we need to become aware of the schemes of the enemy, who is also active all around us. We are at war and prayer is a priority weapon. (See Eph. 6: 10-20 and notice how many times prayer is mentioned!) Of course, Paul consistently mentioned being thankful. Gratitude is our primary response to the grace and the indicators of grace's work in our lives. It is a sort of "grace-o-meter". If you want to be a Christian leader with impact, you need to be in touch with your Leader. He is the Head of the church and initiator in all things. He wants you to have the same relationship with Him that He had with His Father. He did only what He saw the Father doing and He said only what He heard the Father saying. The primary way we see and hear with Him is in prayer. Both in times set aside for prayer and prayer on the way.

God's will for you is to be in continual communion with Him. 1 Thes. 5 : 16 –18 lays this out clearly.

"Be joyful always, pray continually, give thanks in all circumstances, for this is God's will for you in Christ Jesus."

What I have discovered about prayer is that I only pray about what I care about. So maybe our first prayer needs to be for ourselves. Namely, "God change our hearts!" "Expand our circle of concern!" I have no problem praying for my daughter because I love her deeply. If, on the other hand, I pray only about myself, I know there is something wrong. Prayer flows from a changed heart. God's destiny for you is conformity to the image of His Son.

Do you know where His Son is now? At the right hand of the Father interceding! Before we preach to people, we need to pray for people. My first priority is not communicating to them, but lifting them before the throne of grace. Jesus is now praying for the whole world and us. As Christian leaders, we are invited to follow Him and lead others to do the same.

Is prayer a "first of all" for you or "I'll fit it in somewhere, sometime"?

We look at our world and we want it to change.

We look at the people around us and we want them to change.

We look at ourselves and we want to change!

C.S. Lewis said that there are two ways to change the world, "work" and "prayer" and by far the more powerful of the two is prayer. A wise man once said, "When we work, *we* work; but when we pray, God works." Where have we placed our trust?

I believe that God continues to beckon His church to come away with Him. He still wants His house to be a "house of prayer". Will you hear Him and lead His people into this sweet and painful devotion?

Spurgeon, the famous Baptist preacher remarked, "If any of you should ask me for an epitome of the Christian religion, I should say it is in that one word – prayer."

Can you hear the Father calling?

We are speaking to people about having a real relationship with a real person and we must be growing and deepening in that relationship ourselves.

Study Questions

Prayer

1.   Is prayer a "first of all" for you, or "I'll fit it in somewhere sometimes"?

Read 1 Tim. 2:1-6, 1 Thess. 5:16-18 and Col. 4:2-4. What do they teach about devoting yourself to prayer? Where could prayer be better placed in your schedule this week? What will you give away or give up to keep this time free for deeper direction from God?

2.   Lance said his first priority is not preaching to his people, it's lifting them before the throne of grace. How does that compare with how you look at your priorities?

Eph. 6:10-20 calls us to engage in spiritual warfare through prayer. One of the signs of communing with God is how He changes our hearts and expands our circle of concern. What do you sense God wants you to do to deepen prayer for your people?

3.   Get your leaders to pray together as a team and ask, "Lord, how do you want us to fill your church with prayer?"

11   Equip

As I am writing these chapters, I am finishing a yearlong group called Young Leaders' Initiative. It is my simple way of giving away what I have learned over the years in leadership. We meet for two hours once a month, discuss, interact, laugh, and even sometimes cry. We are talking about what leadership really looks like in the real world and the real church. This is what I love to do, and it feels like God is in our midst leading us.

In another chapter I talked about the priority of prayer, so it should be obvious that I think that part of a leader's time should be spent in prayer and meditation. What else does a leader do with their time? What are the roles of a leader? I'll put them in five E's so you can remember them more easily: Envision, Equip, Empower, Encourage and Evangelize.

The Roles of a Leader.

1.   Envision

Leaders paint a picture of a preferable future.

You paint a picture of what the group, organization or church you lead could become. In your mind, what does the dream church look like? What is the Christian life supposed to look like? What is the biblical picture of the abundant life? What is a Christian leader to look like? The ideal marriage? All these subjects and many more are to be envisioned by the leader. The Kingdom leader must have a Kingdom vision for life an. I spell this out more fully in the chapter on vision.

The leader must continually envision his people with a picture of what they could be. Christian leaders are hope givers. They believe in the God of Hope and the power of the God who can change things!

2. Equip

When I was a fairly new believer one of my mentors, Craig, said to me that his philosophy of ministry was to always work himself out of a job. He explained to me that whatever he was currently doing he tried to train someone else to do and then he would move on to another job. He told me not to worry, that there would always be another job to do in the church, since ministry was endless. He was right and he displayed the heart of an equipper.

As I have said, Christian leaders are servants. Our success is the success of those under us. Over the years, I have tried to follow Craig's admonition and it has been quite fruitful.

The church worldwide is in desperate need of more workers and leaders. It is the job of leaders to find and train those workers and leaders. Paul addresses leaders and tells them in Eph. 4 that they are called to equip the saints for the work of the ministry. Our call is to get the rank and file of the church, the regular folk that populate our churches, ready to do the ministry of Jesus. This is God's plan - to reach the world through us. We spend our time serving and equipping the church and they go and change the world.

This means several things. First, we must know how to do the various aspects of the ministry. We can only train people in things we know how to do. That doesn't mean we are equally good at everything, but to have integrity in our training, we must be passing on wisdom we have gained by doing. For example, we can't teach people to pray if we don't pray.

People are trained not just by information. We can't just tell them and they will get it and apply it and do it. It is best to employ a *show-and-tell* method of equipping.

If I want to train someone to pray for the sick, the best way is to take them with me when I pray for the sick. At first, they can watch and observe what I am doing. (Afterwards, ask if they have any questions.) After a few times get them to participate. Down the road, you get them to do it with you watching and you can give them feedback. Eventually you want to leave them doing it on their own. The real win is when they start to do this same process with another disciple. In the Vineyard, we have called this the *discipleship loop*. It combines information, modeling and interaction in the learning process. You can train people in many things like this. I have recently trained preachers with a similar method.

What I want you to see here is that whatever you know and whatever you can do has been given to you so that you can pass it on. So go and work yourself out of a job! There will always be a place for a good equipper.

3.   Empower

When I speak of empowering, I am thinking of two basic things. One is a *supernatural* reality and the other is quite *natural*.

On the supernatural side, we need to do everything we can to get people filled with the Holy Spirit and power. This is the only way they will be able to carry on the ministry of Jesus. He was the prototype of the Spirit-filled Christian. Acts 10: 38 says,

> *"You know of* Jesus of Nazareth, how God anointed Him with the Holy Spirit and with power, and *how* He went about doing good and healing all who were oppressed by the devil, for God was with Him."

We are called to do the same things that He did. People don't have a hope of living life according to this Book and doing ministry as is described there without the power of the Holy Spirit. We are commanded to be filled with the Holy Spirit! (See Ephesians 5 : 18.) We should lay hands on our people and ask God to come and fill them regularly. We need to do this repeatedly. We must create an atmosphere in our meetings where God has room to move and touch and fill our people. God will come if you give Him space and ask Him to come. In the Vineyard we love to pray, "Come Holy Spirit." When we pray we expect God to come and touch and fill our people with the power of the Holy Spirit!

On the natural side, leaders are *permission givers*. We want to empower our people to do what they are called to do. God gives vision to leaders, but within that vision there is lots of room for visions within the vision. I want to create a culture that mostly says "yes" to what the people feel called to do. I want to have an atmosphere that encourages risk-taking and where it is okay to succeed or to fail. Remember, your job is not to control them or keep them in place; your job is to release them to be all they can be in God and do all that He has in mind for them to do. If you have to say "no" all the time, maybe your vision is too small. As leaders we want to empower our people with the Holy Spirit and empower them to do all they are called to do.

4.   Encourage

I hope that the spirit of my church and the movement that I belong to is *"we can do this together!"*

We all need encouragement regularly. A really smart man wrote, "Encouragement is oxygen to the soul." Hebrews tells us we should encourage one another daily. (Heb. 3:13.) I used to think that was extreme. Do people really need daily encouragement? Now my answer is an emphatic "yes!"

There are so many ways we, as leaders, can encourage those around us. You may or may not have figured this out yet, but if you are a leader, people care what you think and say. You have authority on your life so what you do and say toward people is doubly important. Your words and actions can be really encouraging to the folks.

I have written notes to folks pointing out something I like about them or something good that they have done. It literally takes me a minute. Some of them have kept these notes for years. Your words count. Use them to encourage. Catch people doing something right.

You can encourage them by walking with them in the midst of hard times. Even a fifteen-minute conversation full of love can really help someone on their journey.

Encouragement is all about affirming people's being and doing. It is okay to confront and criticize occasionally, but our interaction with people needs to be at least 80% positive, encouraging, and affirming. If people know that you like them and are for them, you can lead them easily. If people think you don't like them and are looking for ways to criticize them, they won't receive much from you at all.

5. Evangelize

This is my last 'E'. I won't take much time with it. I'll save that for another time.

The mission of the church is to carry on the ministry of Jesus. We are His Body and we are to continue to do His work in the world.

His ministry purpose described in the Gospels is "to seek and save the lost."

I know that 90% of the Christian leaders reading this don't feel like they are especially gifted at evangelism, but if we are going to be doing the mission of Jesus in this world we must continue to be engaged in reaching out to a lost and dying world.

Your modeling is huge here. Are you lost in the Christian ghetto? Do you at least have places in your regular schedule to have conversation with those still outside the church? It's not that hard. You can just be yourself.

Jesus doesn't say to try really hard to be the light. He simply says that we are the light of the world. My goal is to be the same at Starbucks as I am in the pulpit. I just want to be me everywhere I go; I am a follower of Jesus, a light in this world.

Paul encouraged his young son in the Lord "to do the work of an evangelist" (2 Tim. 4 : 5). We are to lead the charge to continue the ministry of Jesus. As a leader, you must know that people figure out how serious you are about something by what you actually do.

For the Son of Man came to seek and to save what was lost (Lk. 19:10) To be close to Him is to share His heart for people who have not yet found Him.

You can look at these five E's as a grid to evaluate your leadership. To be effective, all five need to be in place and growing.

Study Questions

Equip

1.   A Kingdom leader has vision for life, ministry, and the corporate body.

Lance suggests 5 'E's' to define the role of a leader. These five characteristics are to envision, equip, empower, encourage, and evangelize. How do you define the role of leader in your church? What picture are you painting for your church to become?

2.   What is the biblical picture of the abundant life and the spirit-filled life? How do you identify these qualities in your rising leaders?

3.   How do you fulfill your call to the rank and file of the church, those regular folk who do the ministry of Jesus?

12   Focus

Ministry is endless and very open-ended.

There are many *good things* to get involved with. I've watched pastors that have spent their days meeting with other pastors, thinking that they would bring unity to the Body of Christ. I've watched the church get distracted by small things and start majoring on the minors. It is enormously hard to stay focused. So how do you stay focused? How do you know how to spend your time, energy and money? No matter who you are, you have limited resources. What do you give yourself to?

As I have said, my primary mentor for more than fifteen years was John Wimber. Many times I heard him use the phrase, *main and plain.* What he was trying to get us to do was to stay focused on the main and plain things taught in the Bible. He was helping us as younger leaders to understand what to focus on. So what are the main and plain things?

It is my considered conviction that the church is meant to carry on the ministry of Jesus. This makes sense to me because we are His Body. We are the primary instrument that He uses to bless the world. We are very important because we are the very place that God resides in on this earth. We are the primary instrument that He is using to redeem the world.

John Wimber often asked his apprentices, "What business are you in?" Jesus has made us His friends and He has let us in on the family business. (See John 15:15.) So it is vitally important to know what business we are in. This gives us, as leaders, our focus. So what business are we in?

There are several ways to answer this, but the phrase we all learned was, *we are in the people-processing business.* We are here to make disciples and everything we do should relate directly or indirectly to that business. If you lose that as your focus, the enemy will keep you in a constant state of confusion and distraction.

Our job is to receive people as they are and make them (with lots of God's help) into fully mature, authentic followers of Christ. A number of years ago I had one of those rare moments of extreme clarity. I heard that still small voice addressing me about my life and its purpose. I sensed God saying to me that my life was simply about *influencing people toward being followers of Christ.* This was focusing and humbling for me. I realized everything I do is toward this end and I also saw that all I could do was influence through teaching, preaching, and by example. Secondly, I was to train influencers, but that is another story.

We find people as they are and give them the wonderful gift of acceptance. We tell them (and mean it) to come as they are and they will be loved, by us and by God. But here we must be honest that although God accepts them as they are, He will move heaven and earth to change them. Our job is to love unconditionally and to cooperate and coach in this big, big transformation of becoming more like Jesus.

As leaders, people come to us in all different states and conditions. Our simple job is to move them along toward the goal. In another chapter, I wrote about a little Greek word in the New Testament that I have come to deeply appreciate - *telos. Telos* means *mature, complete, perfect*; when something or someone reaches the intended end. A person reaches their *telos* when they become what God intended them to become when He created them and recreated them through the new birth. Our job is to cooperate with this process.

In general, God's goal for all of us is to become like Christ, this is our destiny. (See Romans 8:29). But of course God has specific plans and purposes for each member of His Body. As leaders, we can really help people discover who they are and what they are to be about in His larger plan. I often pray and ask God to show me (and them) what He has made them to be and do. I would encourage you to ask for discernment, the ability to read His people correctly.

Non Christian>>>Christian>>>Disciple>>>Worker>>>Leader

People can come to you in any of the above groups. Your job is to move them along this spectrum. Not all will become or are supposed to become leaders, leadership is a gift (see Romans 12:8). I do believe that it is God's heart for all men to be saved (1 Tim. 2:4), for all to become real disciples of Jesus and to find their place in His family and join in the family business. You can be confident of this because it is His stated purpose in the Scripture. So pray and work toward this *telos* in all your people's lives.

Another way to look at the process is in relationship to the church.

Unchurched>>Churched>>Developing habits of discipleship>> Serving faithfully>>Leading (for some)

You get the idea. Your job is to encourage change and growth with this end in mind. It is true of everyone that comes your way and becomes part of your circle of concern and influence.

Different leaders I know phrase this process differently. My friend David Parker uses 3 G's. Their church is trying to Gather, Grow and teach people to Give of their lives and resources.

Another old friend of mine talks about 4 E's: Evangelize, Exalt, Encourage and Empower.

I have used different language over the years. For instance, we have used 3 C's to express God's desire for everyone.

Communion>>Community>>Commission.

We want people to find a real relationship with Christ (Communion), to be safely enfolded into His church (Community), and to be part of spreading the good news (Commission) according to the gifts and talents God has given them. You get the idea.

The way I really think about the process is to begin with the end in mind. What kind of disciples do I desire to make? Then I ask what are some of the key factors to getting folk there? In what way does the life and ministry of Jesus need to be formed in people?

We have six priorities for our church, the Vineyard Anaheim. This is a good starting place for what we want in each of our people.

1. Worship: We want each of our people to live a life of worship, a life that glorifies God
2. Word: We want all of our people to develop a respect for the Bible. Our goal is for people to understand, experience and do the Word. This can only be done by the empowering of His Spirit.
3. Fellowship: We are in this together. God has joined us to a Body and we are to live life together and do ministry together. We are learning together to love God, each other and the world around us.
4. Ministry: The ministry of Jesus is not in one person. His grace has been deposited throughout the whole church. We need each other to serve one another and share the grace that God has given to each of us. We believe we all are ministers.
5. Outreach: We have been given good news and it is for sharing. This is why we reach out beyond our church to plant new churches, to serve the poor, to witness to the lost and to play our part in renewing the larger church.
6. Prayer: Not too long ago God added this to our list of priorities. We believe prayer undergirds everything we do and creates the Kingdom atmosphere in the church.

Each of these areas takes training, encouraging, and envisioning in order to happen. Let me explain for a minute how this works.

What are some of the factors that are key to moving people along in this process? I have watched this process of change happen with hundreds, maybe thousands of people. Here are some of the important things to focus on.

1. Relationship

Ministry and influence flow out of relationship. The more relationship, the more possibility of influence. One thing we have to always remember: WE ARE NOT GOD! We can help people along the process, but each person is responsible for their own spiritual growth.

Remember, we love, and God changes. Nevertheless, your relationship with people as a friend, mentor, father or mother can be a huge help. When I look back upon the people where God has used me the most, I invested a lot of time in our relationship.

2. Knowledge

As leaders, we have the privilege of passing on what it is we have learned. That is hopefully what I am doing in this book! Whatever you have learned over the years in your life and ministry, God will use to bless and help others along their way.

This can be knowledge of the Bible. Don't assume that our people are biblically literate. People today mostly start as biblical illiterates. Give them the pure Word. Model for them how to live it. Wisdom about how things really work is also key to the knowledge that we pass on to others. One of the things I loved about John Wimber is that he was deeply spiritual and yet had very practical wisdom about the church and how it really works.

3.   Personal Responsibility

Everyone is responsible for their own growth. You can't and shouldn't choose for them. You can care deeply about people, but you can't carry them. You can love them and point the way, but they have to walk their own walk. You don't have to try to motivate anyone.

4.   God's Activity

Obviously the whole process of growing up in Christ is totally dependent on God's grace.

You can only participate in what the Father is already doing in a person's life. This means you are to tread lightly and prayerfully, asking God about the next step in a person's growth.

You can get a sense for God's activity in your life and in the life of those you serve. God is always inviting people upward and onward. You can be confident that there is a next step because He is more interested in them reaching their *telos* than you or they are. God will speak to them, coax them, convict them and do whatever else they need to move them forward. He is the Good Shepherd. He has a wonderful plan for people and He is more than able to get them where He wants them to be. He is the great orchestrator and we need to trust in His ability to make disciples (Phil. 2:13).

So when people come your way, your first step is to simply get to know them. Love them for who they are, not for what they should be. Discern what they know and where they are in their process of discipleship. Second, ask yourself, what do they need to do in order to become all that they are to be at the next level? Do they need more information, additional formation or just some gentle encouragement and an opportunity? Third, invite, encourage, and offer to help. Your sheep will hear your voice, as you walk out ahead and respond. May you thrive in the family business!

Study Questions

Focus

1.   Making disciples is the business we are in and everything we do should relate to that business. If you lose your focus, the enemy will keep you in a state of distraction. How do you focus your church on being and making disciples?

2.   People come to us in all kinds of different conditions. Make a list of the things that are hindering your people from becoming mature followers of Christ?

3.   It is important to ask God for discernment and the ability to read his people correctly. Some people are moving towards Christ and others are drifting away. Relationship is critical for influencing them to take another step towards Christ. After reading this chapter, what needs to change in the priorities presented for developing disciples?

13   People

People who need people are the luckiest people in the world?
What do you think?

It is Sunday morning and I have just finished preaching. As I leave
the sanctuary and head toward my car, I am greeted by a very
frantic woman I'll call Bonnie. Bonnie is very, very mad at me,
but not in a private kind of a way. She is screaming at me in front
of many of the people I have just preached to and using words not
fit for this book. Apparently, I had moved her husband's furniture
(it was actually owned by the church) without her permission. I
hate when that happens. (If I told you the rest of this story you
wouldn't believe it. She was one of the most difficult people I
have ever dealt with.)

I haven't seen Jane around lately so I start to ask some questions of
people that know her. It turns out she has gone back to partying,
met a non-Christian guy and has sort of left our church. She now
is not even sure if she wants to be a follower of Christ. I hate that
too!

I received a letter this week from a pastor's wife in Australia. Her
sister has been attending our church and through the sermons and
Alpha, her life is really being transformed. I love that!

I've known Jennifer for a couple of years. She came to the church
through some good friends of mine, Steve and Cindy. Watching
the Lord touch her and change her and her husband has been
nothing short of a miracle. They would say it is. I love that! I live
for that!

I'm sitting in my office with a person on my staff. I've sensed
lately that they are unhappy and unsettled so I'm asking some
questions. Do you feel called to be a pastor? "I don't know." Do
you feel called to our church? "I don't know." Do you feel called

to follow me as the leader? "I don't know." You get the picture. After much more discussion, we both come to the conclusion that they don't fit on our staff and it would be best to resign. A tough conversation. I hate that!

You might be thinking, "Why is he telling us these random stories?" They all have one thing in common: people. **People are the agony and the ecstasy of leadership.** Real people can be a huge blessing or an enormous trial. Either way we can't avoid dealing with people. The church is made up of people. We are in a people business. I've seen young leaders come out of Bible colleges and seminaries thinking that their primary job was to study and teach the Bible. That certainly is important, but they don't count on dealing with real people with real issues that at times can be really difficult or wonderful.

Once a month I meet with some of our county's pastors and this month we met with their wives. We had a nice Mexican dinner together and then gathered in a circle to have a time of sharing and praying. I had a leading as I prayed about the meeting to ask the women only to share. I asked them to tell us what it is like to be a pastor's wife. What do you like? What is really hard for you? Of course, their answers were all about people. They loved to see their lives changed through the church. What was universally hard were the unrealistic expectations that their people put on them. They all said that people were the agony and the ecstasy of their lives as pastors' wives.

From time to time, someone will ask me what is the hardest part of being a pastor? I jokingly respond that it is having 3000 bosses. Everyone in my church has a slightly different expectation of who I am supposed to be. Obviously, if I take their expectations seriously it is a formula for crazy.

We need to remember what real people, even real Christians, are like. I have a phrase I often use to help our people with this. I call

Christians *sinner/saints*. We have been graciously given the status of saint in Christ, but we still sin and we still contend with our old identity and its fleshly habits. No one is perfected, no one is totally healed. My rule is those who are hurting can be hurtful. We share our blessings with each other and we share our pain. The church is a messy business. Like real life! Don't expect Christians to be perfect or even always to be mature. If you have false expectations about real people and how they behave, you won't lead for long. You will end up hurt and disillusioned.

Despite all this, we are called to give ourselves to people. I have seen many leaders over the years become cynical and harden their hearts toward people. They just don't let anyone *in* anymore. Leadership can get really lonely like that.

We always have to remember that the goal of our instruction is love (1 Tim. 1:5). We are called to be an example of love for God and man. I must continue to give myself to real people if I am going to be an effective leader.

Yes, they will disappoint me and yes, they will at times thrill me. Think about Jesus and his guys!

Truth be told, all we have to give in ministry is ourselves. We share who we are, what Jesus has done in our lives, and what we have learned along this journey of life and leadership. Thoreau once wrote, "Rings and jewels are not gifts, but only substitutes for gifts. The only real gift I have is a piece of myself."

Jesus gave Himself and it cost him dearly. We must do the same.

Compared to Jesus, we are a little incarnation of the truth. We are that Word enfleshed again so people can feel and touch and experience His Name.

People can be weird.

People can be wonderful.

Lead with your eyes wide open.

But lead and love and give yourself away.

If you think about it, there is not much on this earth that will survive and transition into the next life. The one place you can invest your time and energy and money to have eternal significance is in God and people.

God bless you with much grace as you relate to the wacky, weird, and wonderful people of God, called the Church.

Study Questions

People

1.　　Lance says to expect sinner/saints not to be mature all the time. Having realistic expectations is important when pastoring people. How do you stay open to your people when they criticize you?

2.　　Read 1 Tim. 1:5. How do you present 'love' to be the goal of your instruction? What does that look like in real time?

3.　　2 Tim. 4:2 reads, "Preach the word of God. Be persistent, whether the time is favorable or not. Patiently correct, rebuke, and encourage your people with good teaching." What insights can you share as a leadership team about how to correct people when it's necessary?

14   Call

When I first arrived at the Vineyard Anaheim, I needed to get to know a rather large and complex church. I spent six months making very few changes and asking a lot of questions. Of course, one of my primary goals was to get to know the staff (at the time, we had about 100 staff of various kinds). I would typically get alone with some of the key staffers and start asking questions. Some seemed happy to be there and some seemed very unhappy on staff. One of the questions that I routinely asked was, "Do you feel called to be a pastor?" (or whatever kind of leader they were.)" Often they would say, "I don't know." "Are you called to the Vineyard Anaheim?" "I don't know." "Do you feel called in this season to follow me, the senior pastor?" "I don't know."

Then I would proceed to explain, hopefully gently, that their responses didn't work for me. I needed a team around me that knew they were called to their ministry area, to this church, and to follow me as God's appointed leader.

I've known for many years that *call* was a big part of someone being successful in ministry long term. Leadership in the church is hard enough and you can only abide in it if you know you are called to do it. If you know you are called to lead, and you are the right person in the right place, you can persevere through many hardships. Paul says, "We must go through many hardships to enter the Kingdom of God!" This is especially true of leaders.

If you are going to step out in front and lead the troops, you can be sure that you will become a target for the enemy. Our call anchors us and sustains us in the hard times. Our success is defined by simply fulfilling the call that God has given us.

Calls can come dramatically or gradually, but they are marked by an assurance, a faith that we are where we are supposed to be, and doing what we are supposed to be doing. Let me tell you a little about my own calling.

A man who was in full-time ministry led me to Christ. At the time, he was primarily doing campus ministry at UCLA. From the day I got saved he took me with him. I just thought that was what all Christians did; they spread the good news that they have received. Linus took me on walks across the campus, ministering to students and eventually on ministry trips to Europe. Within one year of my conversion, I was somehow teaching five Bible studies a week. I don't know what I taught because I didn't know much. I was an avid Bible reader and in the Jesus Movement nobody knew that much, so I taught and evangelized and good things happened and many people were coming to know the Lord.

A turning point in my journey toward leadership came about a year into my walk with Jesus. I was in the hall at my home church, Malibu Presbyterian, when a woman asked me a typical question that you would ask a 20-year-old. What are you going to be/do with your life? All of a sudden, out of my mouth came this strange answer. "If what you guys are telling me is true, what else could I do!" What I meant was, if the good news and the Bible were real and true, then I must spend the rest of my life trying to spread it and influence as many people as possible to be followers of Christ.

Somehow, at just one year old in the Lord I knew that I was going to be in full-time ministry. What had happened to me was so radical that I wanted everyone to share my experience; to receive the eternal life.

The funny thing is, the one thing I assumed is that I would not be a pastor. I didn't relate to the pastors I knew. I couldn't see myself in robes and doing what I perceived they did. I assumed I would end up in youth ministry or campus ministry or some Christian sports ministry. Looking back, this was probably due to the powerful modeling of Linus and his group of friends who discipled me.

I entered an experimental stage. I went to university and seminary and then I determined that while I was there I would try every type of ministry I had the opportunity to try. I did a ton of youth ministry, went on missions trips, worked with sports ministries, and went on faith renewal teams to local churches. I discovered that I liked working with people long term, where I could see what the gospel did in their lives. When I would go on short-term assignments many good things went on, but I often wondered what happened with the people once we left. At the same time, I started to fall in love with the family known as the local church. I started to see that the whole Christian enterprise depended on her.

All the para-church organizations fed off the local church and her members. I realized that people needed the fellowship of the local church to sustain them. It wasn't just Jesus and the individual. We are called into a Body and we are to live and do ministry together. As you might guess, that led me toward being a pastor. I've now pastored in four churches and been in the pastorate thirty-plus years.

What I want you to see is how I realized my call gradually and progressively, especially as I understood myself and what God made me for. Over the years, my call has expanded. I am still pastoring, but I am also a leader in our national movement, and an elder in our tribe, the Vineyard. My latest call has been to write. John Wimber told some of us not to write until we were fifty because we probably wouldn't know anything until then. When I turned fifty, I started getting the desire to write down some of the things that I had been teaching for many years. One by one, friends started coming to me, confirming and encouraging me to write. After church one day someone told me, "The Lord told me to tell you that you have books in you." "Cool," I thought, "another confirmation."

You can be the judge if this is a real call for me.

This is how my call happened, but we are all different, and God deals with us however He sees fit.

For me there were dramatic moments of very specific calling. After one of the very first gatherings of Vineyard leaders, I went home and settled in for the night. The moment my head hit the pillow, I began to have a vision. I saw a map of Long Island. Onto the map came a point and the name Hempstead, which is a town on Long Island. Then I saw a fire fall onto the point and it spread, engulfing the Island. With this momentary picture came the knowledge that I was called to go back to New York and start a ministry that would somehow affect the Island. A year later, we moved back to New York and started one of the first Vineyard churches on the East Coast of the U.S. The church thrived and also planted other churches. I had been very specifically called to a particular place at a particular time for a particular purpose.

Some calls are dramatic and some very low-key and gradual, but an inner knowing that we are doing what our Creator has called us to do marks them all. I personally believe all Christians can have a sense of call no matter what their vocation, but it is essential if someone is going to last in Christian leadership.

If we think of Paul's call, and Isaiah's call, they were very dramatic and radical, but most leaders I know well today had dramatic moments within a gradual assurance that they were called and confirmed as a leader in the church. Ultimately, the people of the church confirm our calling by following us. There are no true leaders without followers, but that is another story....

Study Questions

Call

How is your call gradually evolving?

1.   From a stewardship perspective, the activities I sense God calling me to refocus my life towards are.... Why?

2.   People who know me well believe I am most used by God when I am involved in ....   Why? Though I may have dismissed the thought many times for various reasons, I have felt what I really should be doing is ....   Explain?

3.   When people talk about a passion for ministry, I often begin to think about giving my life to accomplishing .... Why?

15   Humility

Life has a way of adjusting our views of ourselves. My new favorite definition of maturity is *adjusting to reality*.

In the course of my ministry, I have now overseen hundreds of pastors and leaders. Many of them, if not most, come with a false view of who they are. Some see themselves more highly than they should and some see themselves more lowly than they should. Humility is seeing yourself accurately. Not *above* who God has made you, but not *below*. It is not humility to avoid recognizing the gifts, talents, and intelligence God has graciously given you as a leader.

I have a friend named Rich. He is one of the smartest and funniest people I know. He is also very spiritually gifted. He pastors a large church in the Midwest. If he came to me complaining of his lack of intelligence, how he can't discover his spiritual gifts and that he would just like to *amount to something* I would rightfully laugh! That would not be humility. It would be false humility. He would be seeing himself more lowly than he should. An accurate view of him (true humility) is that he is smart, funny, and gifted. Unfortunately, I have lots of friends like this. :o)

I also work with lots of young leaders. Many of them are searching for who they are and what their lives are about. One of the ways to help them is to give them accurate, specific feedback about who they are and what they do. I believe we all build our ministries on our strengths. When folks get that fact, it is a major step in their ministry.

When I first met John, he had a small church that was floundering. As I observed him, I noticed he was a real one-man show. He was doing everything. He pastored a church of under one hundred and he told me they had 25 programs. The people were running like chickens with their heads cut off. They were all up in arms and ready to kill John.

I sat with him in a small restaurant near his church and we began to talk. I suggested to him that he spend the next year only working in his strengths. I asked him to stop doing the things he was bad at and only do what he was gifted to do. John would tell you that this concept was a real turning point in his life. He moved into reality and humility that day. He recognized there are things he did well and others he did not. That is reality and that makes a man humble.

Sam was a new church planter who invited me to South Carolina to spend some time with his leaders. I arrived there and found out that I wasn't preaching, but that he was. That was fine. So I sat back and watched the service. Worship was okay, there were announcements and then Sam got up to preach. For about ten minutes he fumbled around summarizing what he had preached the week before and then for another ten he tried to say something meaningful, but was unsuccessful. After the service was over, I went to lunch with him. He told me that he was such an excellent communicator that he really didn't need to prepare to preach. Inside I was dying! I had just heard one of the worst sermons of my life (and believe me, I have heard many) and he thought it was really good!

Sam was not humble. Sam did not see himself accurately. He saw himself more highly than he should have. If he would have been crushed by his lack of preparation and how badly he had done, I would have been sympathetic, but he obviously didn't see it that way. You may be wondering what I did. Truth is, I did nothing. What I have learned is that life and ministry have a way of bringing people to the truth, to reality. Sam ended up going though tremendous hardship over the next year and it has considerably mellowed him.

Humility is very important for a number of reasons. Humility puts us on God's side. James says that God gives grace to the humble and he resists the proud (James 4:6). If we are going to lead and minister successfully in this world, we need all the grace we can get. We do not want to be in the position of having God resist us! What a horrible thought that we could be ministering in his Name and He is actually resisting our ministry! I live on the ongoing sufficient grace that God gives me in my weakness. We all rely on it. We are in a funny business. We are called to carry on the ministry of Jesus and yet we are totally incapable of doing any of it. We are called to save, heal, and deliver people and we can't (on our own) do any of that! That is humbling. Humility is realizing He is God and you are not. You, even as an extremely gifted leader, can do nothing on your own. You can do nothing that looks anything like the ministry of Jesus.

One of my favorite stories in the Gospels is the parable of the Pharisee and the Publican. You probably know it in Luke 18. The punch line of the story is in verse 14 when Jesus says, "everyone who exalts himself shall be humbled, but he who humbles himself shall be exalted."

If we exalt ourselves, seeing ourselves more highly than we should, God or just life itself will humble us. If we humble ourselves under God, in due time he will exalt us. He will lift us into our proper place in life and ministry. He will promote us and expand our influence as he sees fit.

There are several very practical applications concerning humility in leadership:

1.   Self-knowledge is very important. Calvin said we really only need to know two things. We need to know God and ourselves. When we know who we are, that truth will set us free from frustration and lead us into fruitfulness. We can spend our time and energy doing what God has called us to do and leave the

rest for others. If you are brave enough, ask those closest to you, who really know you, what your strengths and weaknesses are. Depending on your self-knowledge, you may be very surprised at what they say. Just ask them to be gentle and kind. We are all somewhat fragile.

2.	Humility has tremendous implications for team building. At some level, everyone who leads is called to build teams. They may be lay people or group leaders in a smaller church all the way to a multi-layered staff in a big church. What I have learned is that I am not the best at all things. I want to surround myself with people that are good at what I am not. If I am humble enough to realize my strengths and weaknesses and secure enough to have really gifted people around me, we can together build a great team and accomplish some wonderful things for the Kingdom.

3.	Last, but most important, is that you can't have a good relationship with God without humility. Sometimes we act like we know better than God. He is our Friend, but we are not equals. He is the smartest, holiest, best, most well-intentioned person in the universe and He is literally always right. I have watched leaders act like rebels without a clue, thinking they could disobey God and get by with it. He sees all. He is very patient, but He will humble us if we go on exalting ourselves or rebelling. Remember, He loves you and He knows best.

His standards for leaders are high, but they are reasonable and are there for your own safety. Continue to humble yourself under the mighty hand of God.

If we are going to walk like Jesus in this world, we must learn humility from Him. I would like to learn it the easy way, voluntarily, rather than through the school of hard knocks (Mat. 11: 29)!

Study Questions

Humility

1.   We don't want to be in the position of having God resist us. How does humility put us on God's side? Read Js. 4:6 and Lk. 18:14.

2.   How has life or God humbled you? Where have you underestimated your skills in false humility? How are you building your ministry on your strength?

3.   How does humility impact your leadership team? If you are brave enough, ask those closest to you, who know you, to gently share with you what they see are your strengths and weaknesses. How could this information help build your team?

16   Character

All the top leaders of the Vineyard gathered at a nice hotel in Southern California for our annual leadership meeting. John Wimber told us in a previous meeting that he had a serious announcement to make.

He came into the room looking somber and launched into his sad tale. Another leader had fallen. We had started getting reports about him from around the country months before. We heard stories about illicit affairs and emotional attachments, but now they had merged into one big sad story. We all sat in shock as John laid out the sin, betrayal, and deception. It was all very personal to me because he was not only a colleague, but also a friend. John explained that he would be removed from his leadership position, required to go for counseling, and would probably never be in professional ministry again.

One of the most painful experiences I have had in leadership is watching my friends disqualify themselves through their own stupidity and sin. It has been so hard to watch them self-destruct! It really scared me because I realized that none of us are above it.

Character is the number one requirement of the Christian leader.

Gifting is assumed in the life of a leader. God gives certain Christians the ability to lead. All leaders have talent, gifting and at least some level of intelligence, but character is developed over a lifetime. Who we are is the key to longevity in ministry. What we do flows out of who we are.

One way to explain this is that our gifting sits on top of our character.

GIFTING

CHARACTER

The larger the gifting, the more character is necessary to support it.

The more ministry God gives you, the more temptation comes along with it. If you have cracks in your character, the more weight on top of it, the more the cracks will be exposed and the foundation can even collapse! So we need to tend to the cracks as we see them. God will make us aware of the cracks and He is very, very patient, but if we will not deal with the issues of our lives, they will eventually hurt us and potentially many around us.

God is interested in who you are as much as what you do. Gifting can get you into a position of leadership, but character keeps you there. Biblically, character qualifies you for leadership and character can disqualify you. This makes total sense if we think about the role of a leader as an example. We must be credible witnesses to the truth we proclaim.

A word of caution here: None of us is perfect. No Christian leader is perfect. Perfectionism is a trap and can only lead to denial. But we are called to incarnate the truth of the good news. We are called to look and act like the One we follow. We cannot be hypocritical in our person or lifestyle. This call to character, however, must be applied with grace and room for growth. We are all imperfect leaders in the process of maturing.

In 1 Timothy, Paul is instructing his "son in the Lord," about how he should live and minister and how the church should conduct herself. He speaks of the requirements for a leader. It is all about character. There is only one skill mentioned. A leader is to be above reproach or without hypocrisy. No one should look at a leader and say he teaches one thing and lives completely differently. Again, we all have room for growth. Leaders are to have a good reputation in the community. They represent the church in the world.

Committed husband/wife, temperate (balanced), self-controlled – not out of control, respectable – worthy of admiration and imitation, hospitable – welcoming, able to teach (the one skill mentioned), not addicted….. The more pressure the more temptation there is to return to our addictions.

Quite a list!

Paul's whole grid for selecting leaders is character-based. You can teach people leadership skills, but it takes much longer to form character in a person.

The leader is to be gentle, not violent, not quarrelsome or argumentative, not a lover of money – you can't serve God and money – have a good family life, and he is not to be a new believer (although Paul selected elders pretty quickly). You get the point.

Why is character so important to us as leaders?

1.   Leaders influence many people. The have the potential to help or hurt many people. Their lives have a huge ripple effect.

2.   We lead by example. Peter says we lead…. "not lording it over those entrusted to you, but being examples to the flock" (1 Peter 5:3). Our attitudes toward Biblical standards set the tone for our people.

3.   We are qualified by character. See Matt. 12 : 33 and James 3:1. We are not only called to live as a Christian, but leaders have a higher standard!

4.   We reproduce after our own kind. Whoever we are, they (our followers) will become. Whatever we do, they will do.

John Wimber tells the story of a man at a church growth conference asking him how to grow his church to 5000. John asked him, "How many disciples do you want that are like you?" We can't reproduce what we are not.

How is character formed?

This is a big question and I can only begin to scratch the surface. There are five ways I see clearly in the Scripture that God changes us. It is all from Him, but we do cooperate.

1.   Word and Prayer

John 15 promises disciples that they can have eternally fruitful lives, if they do three things. They all center around the concept of "abiding." First, we are to abide in Him and He promises to abide in us. If we will stay close to Him, He will stay close to us. Second, we are to allow His words to abide in us. We must get His words deep down inside of us.   John 17 : 17 says we are changed, made holy, by the truth we find in His Words.

Third, we are to learn to abide in His love. If we do these three things, Jesus says we will have fruit that will remain. Our lives will be significant from an eternal perspective.

The old reformers called these disciplines *means of grace*. I like that. If we avail ourselves of times of prayer and times meditating on His word, they will be channels of his amazing grace.

2.   Modeling

We learn character by watching men and women of character. It is one of those things that are much more *caught than taught*. Paul, in 1 Cor. 11 : 1, makes a bold statement:

"Follow my example, as I follow the example of Christ."

I learned what a Christian looks like as I watched Linus over my first year and a half. I learned what a leader looked like by watching John Wimber for fifteen plus years. Who you are speaks very loudly. If you want to become something or someone, find a person you want to emulate and hang around them.

3. Pain

God uses our trials and our testing to shape us and discipline us. I talked extensively about this in chapter 8. See Romans 5 : 3-4 and Hebrews 12 : 7.

4. Healing

We are all sinners. God rescues us and redeems us and begins to form Christ in us. We all come into this life broken. We all need healing, and leaders are no exception. Thank God that He is the Lord God who heals. We need to get help in our areas of brokenness. Get help for our addictions. These are some of the cracks in our foundation that can ruin a wonderful life of leadership. There is so much help available to us today. Don't be ashamed that you need healing, that you have real issues in your life. You are a real person like the rest of us.

5. Everything!

The wonderful truth is that God uses everything that comes our way to change us and to make us the man or woman that we are to be.

Romans 8 : 28 declares to us, "in all things God works for the good of those who love Him, who have been called according to His purpose."

What many don't understand is what that "good" is?

The "good" we are called to is explained in the next verse. Paul explains that we are "predestined to be conformed to the likeness of His Son."

Let me put this together for you. God uses everything that comes into our lives for our good. That good is that He is changing us, from the inside and the outside, into the likeness of God.

We are being transformed into the image of God.

Day by day God is using everything to shape us and to make us men and women of great godly character.

Here is a wonderful encouraging leadership principal: **God wants to change you and make you one He wants to reproduce.**

So tend your garden. Weed out the things that displease our Lord. Feed yourself with the good things that please the Lord.

Jesus said, "Make a tree good and its fruit will be good, or make a tree bad and its fruit will be bad, for a tree is recognized by its fruit" (Mat. 12 : 33). Be careful what you allow into your mind and heart. I used to tell my Junior High students, "Garbage in, garage out." It is equally true that if you put in good things, good things will come out.

Jesus said, "The good man brings good things out of the good stored up in him" (Mat. 12: 35). My question is: Who stored up the good things in the good man? My answer is: He did!

You have a choice. You can choose what you put into yourself. What you can't choose is the consequences. Put good in and good will come out. Put bad in and bad will come out. If you want to develop good character, feed yourself properly.

Study Questions

Character

1.   The more ministry God gives you, the more temptation comes along with it. If you have cracks in your character, the more responsibility you place on top of them, the more potential for collapse! So we need to tend to the cracks as we see them. How do you safeguard your life from cracking up?

2.   Gifting can get you into ministry, but character keeps you there. We learn character by watching men and women of character. Who in your life do you look up to as someone of character? What qualities impressed you about them? Why?

3.   Read Mt 12:35. You can choose what you put into your life. What you can't choose is the consequences. What is this passage calling out in you?

17 Profile (Picking a Leader)

If you are going to go very far in leadership, you are not only going to lead people, but you are going to have to lead leaders. Leading leaders is particularly tricky. How do you lead people who are used to leading themselves? It all starts with who you pick to lead? What qualities are you looking for in a leader? Over the years, I have selected many leaders. Gradually, I have developed a grid for the kind of leaders I want. As I interview and recruit, I have a loose profile in my mind that I weigh them against.

Just one word of caution before I get to the profile. I am always looking for the leading of the Spirit as I pick leaders. He is the One who knows best who that person is and what they will become. We need to pray for the gift of discernment to know who the right person is for that particular leadership position.

In 1996, I received a word from the Lord. He said to me, "Invest in leaders, present and future, for they are the key." So I asked the Lord to show me the profile of a leader so I could know who to invest in. Here is what the Lord showed me.

1.   Leaders know who they are and who they are not. Self-knowledge allows them to build on their strengths. This knowledge is really important for team building. They can build a team that compliments them and fills in their weaknesses. Humility comes from this accurate self-knowledge, and grace visits humility. This knowing oneself takes time, but you don't want to pick leaders who have a totally false view of themselves.

I once had a leader that came into my office and said to me, "If you and I are going to do this thing together, we need to get a few things straight." At the time, I was the leader of a large church and he was a home group leader. He was assuming he was equal in his leadership to me. Now if that were true it would have been fine, but really he was a low-level leader in our church. He didn't see himself accurately. He thought of himself more highly than he should have. You want to pick leaders who are approaching a realistic viewpoint of who they are.

2. Self-starter. True leaders are motivated internally, not externally. If you have to constantly motivate a leader, you have picked the wrong person. You do need to direct and encourage leaders, especially young ones, but the Lord and his dream for them should motivate them. If you have to stand over people and micro-manage them, you are talking about workers, not leaders. Workers - you tell them what to do and they do it. Leaders - you can work with at the level of vision, the big picture, and then you can let them discern on their own about how to accomplish the vision.

3. Consistent. Here I am looking for people whose life direction is set. They have heard the primary call of being real disciples and they have given their lives to it. They are committed in how they spend their time, energy, and money. They are serious about not just talking the talk, but walking the walk. This doesn't mean they don't have ups and downs, for all of us undulate. But we want leaders who have decided, "As for me and my house, we will serve the Lord."

Christian leaders are first followers and so we want to pick people that have a track record of being serious disciples. People want to follow people who have a consistent core. People like this you can count on. Their priorities are fixed.

4. Called leaders are persevering. Underneath all we do as leaders is our call. We often see the reality of a Christian's call when they experience some difficulty. What happens when they try to gather a group and it doesn't happen or very few show up?

Do they immediately give up or do they start thinking of other ways to get it done? We want leaders who can do nothing else.

Leadership can be a hard and bumpy road. True leaders will be tested, but they will be like the old Timex watch saying, "It takes a licking and keeps on ticking." Those are the kind of leaders I want around me.

5.   Totally committed! We are fond of talking about balance and I think balance is a good concept applied correctly, but here is a dirty little secret. Most of the real leaders in the Body of Christ that I know are not balanced; they are obsessed, even fanatical! They are totally devoted to Christ, to His church, and to His cause in this world. They have given their whole life to following Him and to influencing others to follow Him. They are radical! Leaders must be this: beyond the crowd, beyond the average. We are called to a higher standard. Don't pick a leader that will not go the extra miles to serve the King and His People.

6.   Visionary. (See Chapter 6) A leader needs to be a man or woman of hope: a person who sees a preferable future and has the ability to lead people toward it. True leaders have bigger dreams than the average person does. When you find them, they may have no idea on how to achieve them, but they will have dreams and visions.

7.   Respectable. There are no perfect leaders, but you have to ask the question, "Would you be happy if there were lots of little Jamie's around?" This person has to be worth emulating. Do you like their character? Do you like what they do? Do they live a life that is pleasing to God? Remember, leaders are models. (See Chapter 4.)

8.   Trusted. The beginning of success is not complicated. Successful people show up and keep showing up. Over time, they

become people we can count on. You want to look for people to lead that have shown themselves trustworthy.

Trust is the currency of leadership. That is why it is so harmful when a leader falls. When you stand in front of a group as a leader you are saying to them, "Follow me." When you let them down and prove yourself untrustworthy it can deeply hurt them and the group they are part of. You build trust over time by being consistent and serving people. True spiritual authority comes from ministry.

We shouldn't trust everyone. We should trust those who are trustworthy. We can totally trust God because He is totally trustworthy. To a lesser degree, we want leaders that people can trust, on whom they can really lean.

9.   Otherly. The very first thing I look for in leaders is love. Do they really care about people? That may be displayed in lots of ways according to their personality, but I am looking for a deep caring about the people they are involved with.

Our ministry as leaders is not about us and our successes. It is about the success of others. Good leaders want to see others thrive. They want to bring out the best in others. They see the true potential in every person and are serious about seeing it fulfilled.

True leaders are orchestrators. They are the conductors of the orchestra. They want each player to play well, for the group to play together, and in the end for there to be beautiful music coming out of the group.

10.   Ability to Communicate. All leaders must develop the ability to communicate well. They have to be able to express to others what they have learned. It is their job to articulate the vision they see for their group. They not only need to be a model of the

Christian life, but have to be able to train others to do it as well. I am sure you have noticed that in Paul's list of requirements for overseers the one skill he lists is "able to teach."

We are trying to impart to people a way of life and we desperately need leaders that can clearly explain that way of life to average every day folks.

Now you could probably add to this list many important traits of a leader. So go ahead and make your own list.

Everything in this little book could be on this list. My list is not the point. My point is that you should have your own list. You should have a grid or a profile of what you are looking for in the leaders you are recruiting.

I could have added generosity or being a learner, or loyalty.... or appropriate skill sets for that particular leadership job.

I have given you this profile as a screen, for you to ask of yourself and of those you pick, "Am I a real leader?"

So make your own list. Don't make it too long or you won't be able to hold it in your mind and heart and use it as you look at who you want to invest your life in.

You can't invest deeply in many people and you only have so much time. So choose wisely. Ask the Lord to give you your list.

Happy hunting!

Study Questions

Profile

1.   Lance listed ten criteria he looks for when selecting a leader. They are: humility, self-starter, consistent, persevering, committed, visionary, respectable, trusted, otherly, and able to communicate. As you think about your list, what would you add or change?

2.   What do others that work with you need to know about you? What gets your goat? What thrills you? Which of these qualities do you most cherish in others? Why?

3.   We say "pray for discernment and see what the Holy Spirit is saying" when selecting leaders, but what does that specifically look like? What insights have you learned about selecting leaders? What lessons have you learned, the hard way, that you want others to know when picking leaders?

18   Lasting

I suppose I am about half way through my adult life if I am going to live a long life. I have been a believer for over thirty years and I hope to be a faithful believer and leader for another thirty, God willing. So take this as a sort of "half way" reflection.

I don't take it for granted that a leader will last. I have seen too many leaders' crash and burn. Lots of the wonderfully gifted leaders I have walked with have not continued as leaders throughout their lives. This has caused me to have a healthy amount of fear concerning my own future and a desire to help others to do the things that will help them to run their full race. I share the following reflections with a healthy dose of humility.

Let me get right to it. What do you need to last? Some of the below statements are obvious, but I don't take them for granted any more because I have seen many leaders who do not consistently walk in them.

First, leaders always need to be developing an ever-deepening relationship with Jesus. John 15 paints a beautiful picture of this reality. Leaders need this abiding friendship with their God. We need to learn to walk closely with Him throughout all the ups and downs of leading. Jesus tells us to allow His words to abide in us. Leaders need to learn to meditate deeply on God's word and get it deep down inside of them. Again, I know we know this, but in the busyness of our lives this can easily get pushed to the side. Jesus also tells us in this passage that we need to learn to abide in His love. We have to continue to experience and live in His amazing love. John Wimber used to say that all true ministry comes from intimacy. That is just what Jesus is saying here. An old friend of mine, Kenn, used to say that we need to learn to minister out of acceptance and not for acceptance. God's agape, His unsurpassable, universal, and unconditional love is what He wants us to be at home in. In Him we live and move and have our being, and He is love.

Our very first duty and great privilege is to stay in intimate union with Him. He is the source of our entire ministry and if we get disconnected from our Head, we will soon have nothing to give to the people we love.

Second, you must learn how to respond rightly to hardship. I wrote of this in the chapter on pain. You will not get through your stint as a leader without lots of testing hardship. We need to hold the perspective from Hebrews 12 that hardship is discipline from the hand of the God who loves us.

Two things I would say to you here. First is that whatever you are going through, you must learn to turn toward God and not away from Him. The only way you will make it through all the tests is if you keep turning toward Jesus and asking Him for the grace that is sufficient. If you turn away during hardship, there is only bitterness and darkness. He is the pure source of light and strength. Second, we must always keep in mind the plan. I am referring to the plan laid out in Rom. 8:28 and 29. God takes everything that comes your way and uses it for your good. What that *good* is, is stated in verse 29. We are destined to be conformed to the likeness of His Son.

So remember, God is using whatever is happening to you right now for the good of making you more and more like Jesus. He will use the good, the bad, the beautiful, and the ugly to bring you toward that end. This is your hope at a personal level: that nothing is wasted in God's economy. When I keep this in mind, I can hold on to hope when times are difficult.

Third, you need to continually focus on learning and growing. I love to learn. It is something that motivates and stimulates me.

The Christian life is a way of life that incorporates every aspect of our lives so you will never, ever run out of things to learn.

Many have said that leaders are readers. To that I simply say, "Amen!" We must read in an active manner, really thinking through what we read in order to benefit from it. If you want to understand this better, I recommend that you read, *How To Read a Book* by Mortimer Adler. We have more good reading readily available to us today than ever before in the history of the church, so take advantage of it.

One of my seminary professors at Fuller told the class one day that the hardest thing we would do in ministry is to think. He certainly was right. We have been given the responsibility of helping our people to think through life from a Christian perspective. Of course, this means we need to think through as many areas of life as possible. Our time in meditation can help this, along with the good books we read.

Fourth, we need to continue to take care of our body. Whatever happens to our body affects our ability to function as a leader. But many of us, in a false sense of dedication, neglect or abuse our bodies. We have inherited this wrong view of the body from our forefathers. Martin Luther called his body "Brother Ass." Not a real high view. I understand his sentiment because as I sit here my aging body is in considerable pain and I'm planning hip surgery. But, if you are going to last as a leader, your body will determine the limits of that reality.

It is godly and good to take care of yourself. One of my colleagues who is now in his 60s, told me that a while back he felt like his body was falling apart and he was experiencing lots of pain. Somehow, he discovered that if he stretched daily he felt completely different. He is still vibrant and full of energy for an older guy. ☺ We are whole people – body, soul and spirit – and all of us deserve some care.

As I have become older, one of the realities that I have to consider is the issue of pace. This might have been obvious to a smarter person, but I can't do as much now as I did when I was in my 20s and 30s! I used to be able to go on a ministry trip for two weeks and work day and night and come home and go right back to work the next day. Now if I try that I am exhausted. I need more time to recover. So I have been on this quest to figure out what is a reasonable pace to run at on a regular basis. I have actually thought it through with the help of my counselor and have built a regular schedule for this year. I am trying my best to stick with it. When I do, I am for the first time experiencing Jesus' words about feeling "light" and "easy" (Matt. 11 : 28-30). I've heard it said over the years that it is better to burn out than rust out. But I say I don't want to do either! I want to run at God's pace for me and do only what He has put on my plate to do. I want to live like He really is the Head of my life.

Fifth, it really is okay to have some fun. "Christian" does not have to equal "somber." Many times God has spoken to me through others that I need to learn to play. Even when I am working, I like to incorporate some fun. It is good to develop a regular schedule of retreats and of course be extra serious about a weekly day off. For God's sake, don't take yourself too seriously. Take God and His Kingdom and His church seriously, but learn to laugh at yourself.

Sixth, please build a support system. I always tell my church to build a good system of relationships now, when things are relatively normal, because hard times will come. It is too late to build your support system in the middle of the trial. This really is up to you. You can choose to live in isolation if you want. Press in and develop friends, mentors, and counselors or whatever types of relationship you will need to survive. We can't, and are not made to, make it on our own. Reality and humility teach us we need the support of others. Pride tells us we can do it on our own.

You know that God gives grace to the humble (many times through other people) and resists the proud.

Seventh, if you want to last, you need to find out what you do well and do that a lot. It may take awhile for this to be clear, especially if you are a new leader. Once you find this out, build your ministry on your strengths. God will supply others to do the things you don't do well. They will compliment your weakness. You are not called to do everything. It is absolutely necessary for you to learn to say, "No!" to the things that you are not good at or that you are not called to do.

When you are doing what God has called you to do, you will experience joy in the process.

Spend as much of your time in your strong areas as is possible.

My prayer for you is that you will *last* all of your life, and that you will produce every bit of fruit that God had in mind when He called you into leadership.

Study Questions

Lasting

1. To finish well in life you have to build a good support system of relationships when things are relatively normal, because when hard times hit, you're engulfed in trials. What suggestions offered in this chapter to finish well were the most important? Why?

2. When John Wimber said, "true ministry comes from intimacy." What does that mean? Why is that important to finishing well? How can your leadership team apply that to their ministries?

3. We minister each week to legions of people facing all kinds of painful difficulties, hardships, and bereavements. What needs to be taught in the long obedience so they keep putting one foot in front of the other, their heads down, and taking one more step? Why is this topic one of the most important to teach?

19   Wisdom

It is always a little tricky speaking or writing about wisdom because it seems to imply that I think I am wise and am here to enlighten my audience. I don't feel particularly wise, yet I do clearly see the great necessity for wisdom in the life of any leader. I believe that wisdom is one of the most important qualities of a leader. All of us need wisdom to live a good life, but it is especially important for a leader because of his or her wide influence. Proverbs 4 : 7 says, "Wisdom is supreme; therefore get wisdom. Though it costs all you have, get understanding."

Why is wisdom so important for a leader? Because leadership is about governing and governing requires great wisdom.   Paul, in discussing the utilization of the gifts says, "if it is encouraging, let him encourage, if it is contributing to the needs of others, let him give generously, *if it is leadership, let him govern diligently*, if it is showing mercy, let him do it cheerfully." This is why God was very pleased when Solomon asked for the wisdom to govern. (1 Kings 3)

Let's spend a little time looking at this wisdom. What does wisdom look like and how does it apply to leadership?

James gives us one of the fullest descriptions of wisdom in the Bible in James 3 : 13 – 18.

> *JAS 3:13 Who is wise and understanding among you? Let him show it by his good life, by deeds done in the humility that comes from wisdom. [14] But if you harbor bitter envy and selfish ambition in your hearts, do not boast about it or deny the truth. [15] Such "wisdom" does not come down from heaven but is earthly, unspiritual, of the devil. [16] For where you have envy and selfish ambition, there you find disorder and every evil practice. [17] But the wisdom that comes from heaven is first of all pure; then peace-loving, considerate,*

submissive, full of mercy and good fruit, impartial and sincere. [18] *Peacemakers who sow in peace raise a harvest of righteousness.*

A wise man shows his wisdom by the life that he leads. Wisdom is more than being smart or having a lot of information. Wisdom is the ability to apply knowledge to life.

James shares with us two very unwise attitudes.

1.   "Harboring bitter envy." There is nothing worse than a bitter leader. That leader can easily poison the whole group with their attitude. Many leaders continually struggle with envy. We compare and compete and it can completely rob our peace.

2.   "Selfish ambition." The very beginning of wisdom is the fear of the Lord. As leaders, we must understand that He is God, and He is the Head of the church, not us. We are just under-shepherds given a stewardship over part of His house. Whose kingdom are we building? We can't be builders in God's Kingdom if we are building our own. The devil encourages selfish ambition. What we are doing for ourselves comes from worldly wisdom not from God. A wise person has to understand who they are and who they are not. God is God and I am not!

On the other hand, the heavenly wisdom James describes is a beautiful thing!

1.   It is "pure." You can not see accurately without purity (See Matt. 5 : 8).

2.   It is "peace-loving." A Christian leader is a minister of reconciliation. His job is to bring the alienated into relationship with God and each other (See Matt. 5 : 9).

3.　　This wisdom is considerate and gentle.　The godly, wise leader has figured out that people are fragile and need to be handled with care.　Our people are damaged and need much healing.　We want to contribute to their healing and not damage them further.　Part of this is that leaders need to grow from being purely task-oriented to being more people-oriented.　Besides, God's people are what we are about.

James' description of heavenly, godly wisdom is that it has to do with who we are (our being, character) and how we relate to people.

4.　　This wisdom is "submissive."　This is a real test for my generation (the Boomers), and probably for every generation.　We tend to be rebellious, anti-authoritarian, anti-institutional, and independent.　All of us need to learn to submit.　First, we must practice submission in our relationship with God and second to our God-given human authority figures.　There is truth to the fact that we will never be given real authority until we can accept being under authority.

5.　　"Full of mercy."　Our message is a message of mercy and we of course need to embody that message.　It is just plain smart to give tons of mercy to people knowing that what you give out will come back to you.　This is especially true if you are leading a group of people.　Your attitude will color the atmosphere of the whole group.

6.　　"Full of good fruit."　The wise person knows how to live in a way that pleases the Lord.

7.　　"Impartial, unwavering, sincere" (without hypocrisy).

We must have wisdom to govern well.

Every leader has to make decisions. As you go on in leadership, this becomes all the more true and significant. We need God's wisdom to make good decisions. As leaders, we also will be called upon to help solve problems. This is a wisdom issue. We need wisdom for knowing the next step. One of the ways to see wisdom in the book of Proverbs is learning to see the end from the beginning. Now, only God can do that completely. But as a leader, you are called upon to chart a course for the group you lead. We need wisdom to be a lamp unto our feet to at least know the very next step. We constantly need to seek God for His help and wisdom. Even as we teach, we need wisdom. It is one thing to accurately explain a passage of Scripture, but it is a much more difficult thing to help people understand what that Bible passage has to do with their lives. Wisdom helps us apply the Scripture to our listeners in a helpful way.

Wisdom also helps us to see the bigger picture. We have to understand the whole story of the Bible in order to understand the parts. Wisdom helps us to see the whole counsel of God and to see its part in balance. Wisdom is required in selecting leaders and many other portions of our job. All this to say, leaders really need a great deal of wisdom to function effectively.

God is the source of all wisdom.

We receive wisdom on our knees (See James 1 : 5).

God freely offers us wisdom if we will simply ask Him. I believe it is His desire for us to grow in wisdom all the days of our lives. If we will keep seeking, we will keep finding.

All Christian leaders should be perpetual inquirers. If you study the kings of the OT, you will notice something very important about them. The good kings "inquired of the Lord", the evil kings looked elsewhere. It is so important that we spend regular time listening, and asking the Lord about the issues that confront us daily. Please practice listening for direction and input. Your own counsel will be inadequate for your life and ministry. God has set this up so we are completely dependent on Him. Jesus says we can do nothing without Him.

We receive wisdom as we study and meditate upon the Word. We get wisdom as we pray. We can receive wisdom from other godly men and women either in person or through their books. We should and will learn from others, but remember that only God knows your exact situation fully and therefore only He knows exactly what should be done.

Wisdom starts with our own lives, but it extends to what we do with our lives. God wants to make Christian leaders into master builders that cooperate with His work in the world.

Paul says, "by the grace God has given me, I laid a foundation as an *expert builder*, and someone else is building on it. But each one should be careful how he builds" (1 Cor. 3 : 10). Paul was a wise, even expert builder, and he encourages us to build with wisdom as well.

What we build as Christian leaders is all about Jesus. He is the foundation of the church and everything she does. We must major on Him! It is so easy to get side-tracked on some lesser doctrine or theme. Invest yourself in God's priorities. He says it is about loving Him and loving people. Invest your time, energy and money in God and people, for that is what will last eternally.

A good place to glean some of Paul's wisdom about leadership is to spend time in his letters to Timothy and Titus. There we see the advice he gave to young pastors concerning their own lives and the churches they were called to lead.

Here is a little advice for those who would lead wisely. First, unless the Lord builds the house, you labor in vain (Ps. 127). All you can do is cooperate with what God is building, nothing more and nothing less. He does include us, but He is the senior partner. Always remember He is the Head of the church and He wants to initiate what goes on in her. So we build, one command at a time, knowing that He has a unique plan for us and our group.

When I was pastoring on Long Island, we had outgrown our facility and were looking for a larger venue. We looked for a long time and were about ready to give up. One morning I was praying, and the Spirit whispered to me, "Build a house for the poor and I will build you a house." When receiving words from God many times they come with a certain understanding of what they mean. I knew that if we would obey God and invest in a house for the poor, He would provide us with a place to house our church. We spent some time finding out who the poor were on Long Island and we discovered they were primarily women with children abandoned by their spouses for one reason or another. So, we bought a house that we could use to minister to these women and children, helping them transition toward self-sufficiency. We called it our Parish House and it is still in operation some fifteen years later. Not long after we spent all our savings on this house, I received a call from a realtor representing a Baptist church nearby. They were going out of business because they had shrunk down to nineteen members. They wanted to know if we would be interested in their building. They came and visited us on a Sunday, saw all the young people we had reached and then did everything they could to help us into their facility. They gave us their building for about a third of the market value with very little down. They were amazing and represented the best of the church in their generous attitude.

My point, of course, is that God directed us in an unusual way. He called us to give away what we had saved and then provided in a completely unexpected way. His ways are not our ways. He is way smarter than any of us combined. We are extremely privileged to get to participate in His wisdom in His world. We need wisdom. He has wisdom. He loves to share.

It seems right to end with something really practical on this subject. Let me explain briefly some of the main ways we acquire wisdom:

1.   From the Word. We need to get His Word deep down inside of us (John 15 : 7). The Word will show you the next step in your journey (See Ps. 119 : 105). We store it up inside of ourselves so the Holy Spirit can access it at the appropriate time in our lives and ministries.

2.   From the Spirit. We should constantly ask God for words of wisdom as we confront the various issues in our lives and in the lives of those we lead. Of course, this means time listening and praying.

3.   Hanging out with the wise. Much of wisdom is caught, not taught. Just being around wise people and seeing how they do life will really increase your own wisdom. Don't be afraid to ask them lots of questions. Be bold. Many older leaders want to be asked! If you can't be with them directly, read their books and listen to their tapes. A book is a wonderful thing. You can glean what the author has learned in a lifetime in just a few hours.

4.   Experience. God is growing you up. He is using everything that comes into your life to mature you (see Romans 8 : 28 – 29), so pay attention to your life. God is always at work in and around you. It is good to ask periodically, "What is the Father doing in me in this season of my life?" The seasons of your life will shift and change, so pay attention.

5.   Gifting. Some people are just gifted with lots of wisdom. They just seem to know how things really work. All of us can

grow in wisdom, but it would be a valid request to continue to ask God for the gift of wisdom.

6.	The World. Wisdom is both a Biblical and a public issue. Wisdom cries out in the streets! There is much wisdom out and about in the world. We can learn a lot from leaders in and out of the church. We can learn from people that are not Christians. As we seek to learn from the world, we simply must exercise discernment. Truth is truth and it cries out everywhere for the discerning. Ultimately, wisdom includes everything in this whole wide world. All wisdom and all truth ultimately come from our Creator (see Proverbs 1 : 20).

May the Lord give you great wisdom as you seek to lead His people.

Study Questions

Wisdom

1.   A wise man shows his wisdom by the life that he leads. Solomon, for all the wisdom he was given, did not finish well (see 1Kings 11:1-13). What does James 3:13-18 teach you about applied wisdom?

2.   How has "bitter envy and selfish ambition" caused strife in your leadership over the years?

3.   How will you teach these seven principles of heavenly wisdom to your church?

20 Mystery

We must recognize that there is a certain mystery about leadership. I've seen leaders do all the right things and fail miserably. I've also seen leaders do all the wrong things and succeed anyway. At best, leadership is a cooperative venture between you and God. What is hard to figure out is where your part begins and ends. What is God's part and what is the leader's?

Jesus said, "I will build my church" (Matt. 16 : 18).

The Psalmist says, "Unless the Lord builds the house those who labor, labor in vain" Ps. 127.)

Yet, Paul says in 1 Cor. 3 that he is a *master* or *expert* builder. He claims to be a builder in God's church.

Does God build or do we build?

It takes some wisdom to figure out what is God's side and what is ours. This is really important because we don't want to assume God's role and, on the other side, we don't want to fail to do what is our part.

The mystery happens when our part and His part come together. We are definitely the junior partners in this venture of building His church. He is Head and He initiates, but we do have our part. He has chosen us to play a vital role. We can't do it without Him and He won't do it without us. We must be very clear that we can't grow the church, but we do have our assigned tasks. Paul sows, Apollos waters, but only God can give the growth!

Let's look for a moment at what Paul, our expert builder did to build:

1.   **He prayed!**   And he prayed and he prayed.

Paul mentions prayer at the beginning of many of his letters and often says he prays for them constantly. Paul was a man of prayer and believed that somehow God used his prayer to build the church of Jesus Christ. He instructed his son in the faith, Timothy, to make prayer of the first importance (1 Tim. 2 : 1ff). He told the church in Thessalonica to pray constantly (1 Thess. 5 : 16 – 18). Paul, knowing that only God could add to the church and mature the believers, prayed for them a lot. God wants his church and the lives of his leaders *full of prayer*. As I have traveled over the last few years, I have often heard God say to his church, "fill the church with prayer." Read the book of Acts and you will quickly see this reality in the first century church.

2.   He taught the whole counsel of God.

In order for the church to be healthy, it needs a balanced diet. Paul not only taught his churches the simple Gospel, but every aspect of the will of God that he understood. In his writings, we see a wide range of subjects addressed. It has been my dream to have a fully orbed church that expresses the full-blown Kingdom message. His Kingdom is meant to touch every area and aspect of our lives.

If you think about your church or group as a garden in which you want a wonderful variety of vegetables and flowers to flourish, then it is obvious you can't just plant one type of seed. You need lots of different seeds to grow lots of different types of plants.

3.   He continued to proclaim the Gospel.

Paul, as an apostle, had a very unique role in gospel proclamation, but we have a role in this no matter what our unique gifting is. At the very least, make sure that your people know Christ. Don't assume that everyone in your group is a Christian. Continue to preach the basic Good News. Weave it into your teaching constantly and give folks an opportunity to receive Christ.

Paul told Timothy to continue in the role of an evangelist. We are a good news people and you, as the leader, must be the primary example of this.

It is also good for a leader not to get too locked behind the walls of his own church. Find some place where you can relate to people outside the church. This could be as simple as going and hanging out at a Starbucks. Or you could do it in an area of interest where you live.

You just need to be somewhere on a regular basis where you can have conversations with people outside of the church.

4.   Paul trained and appointed leaders.

Paul built the church by multiplying himself in other leaders. Sometimes he spent lots of time with them like young Timothy or Titus, and sometimes he appointed them rather quickly. I believe Paul quickly discerned in a group who the elders were and just appointed those who God had already called to those positions.

The Kingdom is extended by daily adding to the church those who are being saved. The Kingdom is multiplied every time a new leader is recruited and trained and released into the church. Paul knew that whatever time he spent with leaders would have a far-reaching effect on the church and the world. Knowing this is true, he spent time coaching leaders in how to build the church. If you want to see a great example of this, see Paul's letters to Timothy and Titus. My mentor, John Wimber, taught us to do this with a simple 5-part outline. He taught us as leaders of leaders that this was our primary job. We were to: 1 – Recruit, 2 – Train, 3 – Deploy, 4 – Monitor, and 5 – Nurture. This process would guarantee that we would pass on whatever we know to the next generation of leaders. One of my early Christian friends always used to say that his job was to work himself out of a job. I like that.

So here is a little checklist of things on your side of the equation. These are the things that are your job description.

- Are you praying for your people?
- Are you teaching them the whole counsel of God?
- Are you continuing to proclaim the Good News of Jesus Christ in and out of the church?
- Are you multiplying yourself in younger leaders?

If you will faithfully carry out your side of the mystery, you know God will always be faithful. Just make sure that what you are involved with is not just a good idea, but a God idea. You want to be involved with extending His Kingdom with His Power and for His Glory. You will need to be as sure as you can be that He is the Head and initiator of your group, project or church.

Building the church is a mysterious alliance between the leader, his/her people and God.

Study Questions

Mystery

1.   Prayer and applying God's Word is a mystery of the Spirit. It's a cooperative venture between you and God. The mystery happens when our part and His come together. Read 1 Tim. 2:1 and 1 Thess. 5:16-18.

Why do you think God is calling for more prayer today? What would it look like if you filled your church with prayer?

2.   Mt 28:19-20 instructs us to "teach to obey all that I commanded you." Proclaiming the gospel includes the entire story.

There are three issues this chapter brings up for us to discuss as a leadership team:

1. How do you teach your people to apply what you give them?
2. What is your plan to bring them the whole counsel of God?
3. What do you do to intentionally multiply yourself in younger leaders?

3.   If I were new to your church and asked, "How do I share the gospel in and out of this church?" What would you tell me?

4.   There are five aspects to leadership:

1-recruiting,
2-Training,
3-Deploying,
4- Monitoring and
5- Nurturing.

Which are your strengths and which are your weaknesses? What could you do to shore up your weaknesses?

21   Communication

My sister, Alison, says I have the gift of the gab. I don't know. She says I have always had it. It's so hard to tell if you are a good communicator because good communicators come in lots of shapes and sizes. Communication, like leadership, is more of an art than a hard science. You can communicate in lots of styles as long as they fit you. I want to briefly share ten things I've learned along the way as I have communicated in many settings from one-on-one, to small groups, to very large gatherings.

Test them out and see if they are true.

Communication is an essential element of all leadership. You can't lead effectively without becoming pretty good at it. This is true whether you are a parent or the CEO of a major international organization. Here are a few morsels to chew on as you seek to become a better communicator.

1.   Know your target audience.

I am often asked to speak at conferences and I frequently end up speaking in the very first session. This is extremely difficult at times, because I don't know the people and they don't know me. As the conference goes on and I get a better feel for the group that I am addressing, it becomes easier and easier to speak to them in a meaningful way.

Now we are all people with some needs and wants in common, so you can speak to anyone with some effect, but the better you know your audience the more *on target* your communication can be. This happens primarily through long, hard listening. We want to listen to the people asking lots of questions, and listen to God's Spirit for He knows exactly what that group needs at this time and season. What I am saying is, one size doesn't fit all here. You need to tailor, or at least adjust, your communication to the specific group. In some ways, this is so obvious. You would never address a kindergarten class the same as a group of pastors. (Although sometimes it seems appropriate!)

This is one of the reasons I like pastoring the same church for a long time. I get to know the people and their life situations and can help them in a very direct way.

2.   Know your communication style.

Your style must fit you. It should fit your personality. I believe there should be a connection between how you are normally in daily life, and how you are before a group. This gives you a certain integrity and sense of being real. Your style can take years to develop. There is not a problem with picking someone who you like and emulating them, but eventually have your own unique voice and your own unique delivery.

My only goal here is to keep improving as Lance *the communicator*. No need for comparing or contrasting myself with others, only to give constant work and improvement to my communication.

3.   Always try to communicate with integrity.

If you are with a group for a weekend, you may get away with not being completely honest, but if you live with the people, they will see through you. I recommend real honesty. We present God's ideals and then we share that we are like everyone else in process. We are God's workmanship; His poem in process. We are not yet fully written. If you will dare to be honest about your weaknesses, it will communicate a powerful message of grace to your audience. There is a great temptation to embellish and exaggerate as you tell your stories. We think at times that it makes the stories better and more powerful. But once people figure out this is what you do, you will lose much needed credibility in their eyes.

Simple and straightforward with great honesty is the best!

4. Humor is a wonderful and necessary thing.

I suppose I should tell a joke here, but I'm trying my best to keep
this brief. Humor is the pause that refreshes. Especially if you are
dealing with an intense subject, humor can give people a mental
break before you go on. Humor raises your rapport with the
people that you are speaking to.

Self-deprecating humor is a crowd favorite. It shows them you are
not taking yourself too seriously. As a Christian leader, I want to
take Jesus really seriously and His truth with the utmost sincerity.
But I want to maintain the ability to laugh at myself and let the
group in on the joke. I'm just like they are.

Maybe a warning is appropriate here. Too much humor can
actually make you ineffective. People can remember you were
really funny and totally miss what you are trying to say.

I will tell a joke occasionally or read some funny lists, but my
favorite type of humor happens spontaneously. If you are quick
enough on your feet, it can lend to a wonderful moment between
you and your audience. It becomes a time of play that you share.

5. Storytelling is one of the most powerful communication tools.

We can all remember stories. Jesus was the best communicator
that ever walked the face of the earth and He often told stories. He
was a master storyteller. The best scholars tell us that His stories
(parables) usually had one point. I would say to you - make sure
you know the point of the story you tell and how it connects with
the rest of your talk. Don't make the story so long and complex
that the people miss the point. Sometimes, Jesus gave the point in

a clear punch line, and sometimes He left it to His listeners. I would encourage you to make the point somewhat obvious.

Stories are a great way to illustrate and fill out your communication. Like humor, they can be over used. A few good stories are preferable to many *so-so* stories that sort of relate.

Some of you are naturally gifted storytellers and the rest of us have to work at it. I would encourage you to practice telling the story until you tell it well. Tell it to your wife or friend and see if it makes sense to them.

6. Simplicity is vital to communicating effectively.

Maybe you have experienced the same thing that I have when listening to a person give a sermon. At the end of the sermon, I am impressed with the person, their knowledge, and all the things they brought, but I can't remember the main point. What was being communicated?

Remember that people can only take home a small amount from one sitting. Therefore, I have to ask myself, "What do I really want them to learn today and take home with them?" I want to be able to say it in one sentence. This becomes my goal for that communication session. If you give people too much, they will tend to get frustrated and take home nothing. It's like trying to give them a drink with a fire hose.

My rule is that if you or I can't say it simply, maybe we don't really understand it ourselves

Pretty smart people make things complicated. That may even impress you. Really smart people take complex things and make them simple so that we can understand and apply them.

7. When you are giving a talk, logical progression or structure is important.

You must learn to make simple logical outlines. If you are teaching from a biblical text, you can use the outline of the text itself. Or you can organize your talk around your one big idea with some sub-points. There are many ways to do it, but it must make sense to you and your audience. Rabbit trails are frustrating and distracting to your listeners. I would think this through early on before you illustrate and amplify and fill in your talk.

8. Please know your material!

Don't wing it hoping God will bail you out! You must study adequately to know your topic or text thoroughly. It is embarrassing to you and your group, if they care about you, when you are not prepared.

One way to think through a topic or text is to ask as many good questions of it as you can. Then your research simply becomes answering the questions. Here we try to anticipate the audience's questions and answer them.

Don't make statements that you are not sure of. It is okay to leave something out of your message if you don't understand it or are not able to articulate it well. Better to give them a few things you are sure of than lots of conjecture.

It's even okay to be honest about your ignorance. People appreciate a simple "I don't know." If I am communicating in a Q & A setting, I will often introduce it by asking for permission to say "I don't know" when it is true.

9. Apply. Apply. Apply.

In my humble opinion, application is the element most missing in the communication of the church today. We simply must do better here. People need to know that what we are saying touches their daily lives. We must help them to know how to work this all out. Sometimes we leave people feeling good, or not, but with no idea what Sunday has to do with Monday.

Here are a couple of key questions to test your communications:

- What does this have to do with the people I am addressing?
- What if they believe me? What difference would it make?
- So what? I like this one! When I am done preparing I have to ask myself honestly – so what?
- How does this big idea, my one main point, touch the lives of these people and me?
- Finally, here is a big question for integrity sake. Have I applied this truth to my own life? It doesn't have to be fully worked out for as I said, we are works in progress, but there needs to be some reality of it for it to have any real weight behind it.

There is a monumental difference between what I research and present and truth that has become part of my life. My experience is that God empowers that in an entirely different degree. It just comes out real.

10. Remember to balance affirmation and confrontation.

Everyone you know needs lots of encouragement. By pastoring all these years, I have learned that this is unquestionably true. This encouragement can come through affirmation or confrontation. Everyone is difference here, and some are moved more by one or the other, but I would say that most of the ratio needs to be about 80/20. People need way more affirmation than confrontation.

People can hear hard things from you if they know you love them and want the best for them.

If you are always focused on a person or group's negatives, eventually they will shut you off. So I would make the tone of your communication as encouraging as you honestly can. Find out their strengths and affirm then. Catch them doing the right thing and point it out.

All we are trying to do is help people to grow, so affirm what is right and gently confront what is wrong, knowing that you are in the same boat as them.

If you are going to be a leader for the rest of your life, you will have to learn to communicate in a more and more effective manner. This is indeed very challenging.

Obviously, there is more than one side to this communication. My ten points focused mainly on our side of the communication, but I could say much more about how people listen. I am sometimes amazed at what people hear from what I said. Sometimes it is mysterious and amazing when the Holy Spirit takes what I say and applies it to the listener in a way I would have never anticipated. Sometimes they simply miss the point. Even if you were the perfect communicator, there is the whole other side of the hearer.

You are not responsible for what people hear. That is between them and God.

Jesus the perfect communicator was often misunderstood. So keep trying, this is not a perfect science.

My hope is that you can use these ten little thoughts the next time you have to give a talk or even have a significant exchange with a person. See if they hold true to you.

Study Questions

Communication

1.   Take Lance's communicator checklist. Ask your spouse or best friends to evaluate your communication style.

Rate the following with either: E= Excellent, G = Good, N= Needs improvement.

_____ Adjusts well to your target audience
_____ Understands their communication style
_____ Communicates with integrity
_____ Uses humor effectively
_____ Good Storyteller
_____ Lays out simple points
_____ Organized and easy to follow
_____ Is rehearsed well for clean presentation
_____ Focused on application and ministry time
_____ Confronts hard issues in a loving tone

2.   How do you want your communication style to evolve over this next year? How will you resource this change? Who do you like to emulate? What is it about their teaching you like?

3.   What other mediums are you trying to employ to enhance application and response to your teaching? How could you employ more creativity in the way your entire service comes to be?

22   Final Thoughts

Thanks for reading through to this point. I hope you enjoyed the ride. We have covered a wide range of subjects from ideas about who we are called to be, to what we are called to do.   Each subject could be a book in itself! My hope and prayer is that you could learn some of the lessons I have learned in the past 30 years.

I originally named this material Lance's Lessons on Leadership, but I later thought this is not completely true.   These lessons where taught to me by others like Jesus, Paul, Linus, John Wimber and even some Christians I have never met like John Calvin. I am really just another link in the chain of leadership in the church of the Living God. I am just one more apprentice trying to learn to follow the Master.

I called this book Simple Thoughts on Leadership because I wanted to give you truth in a nugget form, a simple form.   I hope these simple ideas can be taken and personalized and unfolded by others smarter and more gifted than myself. May God bless you in your pursuit of him and in becoming the best leader you can be.

May you know Him and the power of His resurrection and be willing to share in the fellowship of His sufferings. Please pray with me for God to call and equip many more leaders throughout this world. The church can do anything if it has sufficient leadership.